T0067196

PHYSICAL TO METAPHYSICAL IN FOUR STEPS AND ONE GIANT LEAP

MICHAEL K. YEN

BALBOA.
PRESS

A DIVISION OF HAY HOUSE

Balboa Press books may be ordered through booksellers or by contacting:

Balboa Press
A Division of Hay House
1663 Liberty Drive
Bloomington, IN 47403
www.balboapress.com
1 (877) 407-4847

Because of the dynamic nature of the Internet, any web addresses or links contained in this book may have changed since publication and may no longer be valid. The views expressed in this work are solely those of the author and do not necessarily reflect the views of the publisher, and the publisher hereby disclaims any responsibility for them.

The author of this book does not dispense medical advice or prescribe the use of any technique as a form of treatment for physical, emotional, or medical problems without the advice of a physician, either directly or indirectly. The intent of the author is only to offer information of a general nature to help you in your quest for emotional and spiritual well-being. In the event you use any of the information in this book for yourself, which is your constitutional right, the author and the publisher assume no responsibility for your actions.

Print information available on the last page.

ISBN: 978-1-5043-8041-6 (sc)
ISBN: 978-1-5043-8043-0 (hc)
ISBN: 978-1-5043-8042-3 (e)

Library of Congress Control Number: 2017907380

Balboa Press rev. date: 05/23/2017

Touch the outer moon, one small step
Grasp the Inner Sun
One Giant Leap

Dedications

To my parents: without their physical contribution, I would not have lived to write this book.

To my wife, Cathy: without your emotional support, I could not live here long. You saved my life.

To my sister, Melanie: you taught me things I did not know and could not have learned from anyone else.

To my mentors, Professor Shen Heyong and Professor Gao Lan: no words... only gratitude.

To my brother, Stan: it is not whoever dies with the most toys win, but how you played!

To my brother, Raymond: you taught me to aim high and how to tie my shoelaces.

To my personal hero, Mr. Thomas Campbell: your TOE is the biggest!

To my former lovers: as you read this, know I have grown up (a bit).

To my brother-in-law, Harry: you already know how this is.

To my brother-out-law, John: you are the hardest one of all.

To my nephew, Sean, and niece, Marina: this is for you, and the generation that will make a new world...

To my readers: please look before you leap, then take one giant one!

To my editor and friend, Joy: I offer these words from 'Abdu'l-Bahá, "Joy is the best cure for your illness. Joy is better than a hundred thousand medicines for a sick person. If there is a sick person and one wishes to cure him, let one cause joy and happiness in his heart." You do that for me and so many others...

Table of Contents

Introduction

The dawn of human consciousness is generally agreed by archeologists and historians to be impossible to pin down in time or place, an event lost to the mists of antiquity. What artifacts and remains we do have indicate that the emergence of several external behaviors signified giant leaps in our ancestors' inner life: use of fire, symbolic language, (and in my view, the first giant leap) the making of new tools that previously only existed in the mind of its creator. I believe tool making had to be the first breakthrough because many animals have been observed using found objects as tools or even fashioning them into better tools, but in such instances, it is simply making minor modifications to the object rather than a breakthrough involving "seeing" the tool within an object or combining several objects into a new tool.

Use of fire involves modifying the physical environment as well as an emotional breakthrough to overcome the fear of fire, and no animal has been observed to use fire in a proactive way. Symbolic language involves high level abstractions and coordination of physical, emotional and intellectual abilities. Certain marine mammals and some chimps appear to be able to learn to use it from humans, but it remains an open question whether we are the only creatures on Earth that appear to be inherently capable of it. However, the true hallmark of human consciousness, self-awareness, involves integrating other aspects of "being" than just our physical, emotional and intellectual aspects.

All of known history can be seen as our continuing struggle to better cultivate and refine our physical, emotional and intellectual resources. The globalized culture and civilization we see today is the result of this collective struggle, and there is mounting evidence that we have taken a wrong turn down the path of societal development. Sociological and technological development has grown in wildly unbalanced ways. Poverty and exploitation are rampant. Pollution and ecological disasters are ever increasing. The emotional well-being and psychological health of individuals are sacrificed for the financial gains of corporate elites, and yet no alternative model seems to be able to compete with this current dominate model of development.

Though aware of these facts, few seem able to fathom an alternative approach. Yet, the reasons these things are happening and accelerating are not unknown. In fact, they have been known for a very long time: excessive materialism leads to corruption leads to a collapse of society. But how did materialism become the dominant way of understanding our existence here?

When René Descartes declared that "I think therefore I am," he implicitly reduced the mind to a kind of matter, *i.e.*, a thinking substance. And when Isaac Newton declared that "God in the beginning formed Matter in solid, massy, hard, impenetrable, moveable Particles... so very hard, as never to wear or break in pieces," many people turned science into a form of materialistic religion. Anything that wasn't Matter didn't matter.

Then Darwin introduced Newton's materialism into biology with the maxim "survival of the fittest," and inheriting desirable traits became seen as the essential purpose of life. In Social-Darwinism, greed and accumulation became viewed as the natural virtues of society, separating one individual from the next, one country from the next, and humans from all other species.

In this way, all aspects of life were affected. The physical sciences had nothing to do with ethics, philosophy had nothing to do with the arts, and the order of the universe had nothing to do with the way in which we should live. In such a world, Jacques Monod advised "Man" to wake up to "his total solitude, his fundamental isolation. He must realize that, like a gypsy, he lives on the boundary of an alien world; a world that is deaf to his music and as indifferent to his hopes as it is to his suffering or his crimes." No ghosts, no gods, and not much good.

In this totalitarian materialistic environment, let's have the courage to remember that our physical reality is actually guided by a system of unseen forms (or conceptual entities) which are so powerful that even though they don't carry any mass or energy, they are actually the only permanent reality. I say remember because this is knowledge that was available a long time ago.

The ancient Taoists posited that all creation emerged from Nothingness, an unimaginable Void beyond the vacuum of outer space and unfolded into the seemingly infinite physical manifold we see around us. The ancient Greek philosophers saw an underlying reality of perfect forms from which our physical world is projected. The major revealed religions all teach that this earthly life is but a preparation for the real world of the spirit. Numerous classical great thinkers have variously come to very similar conclusions – WHAT APPEARS MATERIAL IS NOT REAL, REALITY IS NOT PHYSICAL.

In modern times, Carl Jung rediscovered the psychic system of archetypal reality that underlies human experience and made many insightful observations on the linkage between inner experience and outer reality. As it turns out, Carl Gustav Jung's revolutionary views of the human mind are in perfect agreement with the discoveries of Quantum Physics which, during the last century, revealed the fundamental errors of Classical Physics and are slowly leading to a need for radical changes in the materialistic view of the world.

The quantum phenomenon forces us to see that the basis of the material world is non-material, and that there is an underlying realm of the world that we can't see because it doesn't consist of material things, but of non-material forms. These forms are real, even though they are invisible, because they have the potential to appear in the empirical world and to act on us. They form a realm of potentiality for the physical reality, and all empirical things are emanations of this realm.

There are indications that the forms in the cosmic potentiality are patterns of information without even the least bit of physicality. Physical reality, in this view, is really a virtual reality. Individual personalities in it interact as data streams joining together like avatars in a Larger Consciousness System (LCS). Religious scholars might prefer to describe this view of material reality as everything and everyone being "thoughts in the mind of an omnipotent God."

However one chooses to phrase such a view of reality, the common thread that runs through them all, is that this view, sees all the parts appearing separate and interacting separately, but are in fact inextricably linked. In the quantum view of things, the world appears as an undivided wholeness in which all things and people are interconnected and consciousness is a cosmic property.

What I propose is that we can in our own experience of reality obtain proof that this is indeed the truth. We can directly access the decreasing physicality of "what is real" by observing our physical, emotional, intellectual, and energetic aspects, and ultimately touch the cosmic wholeness that we are all a part of. As a Jungian analyst, I am familiar with working in psychic systems of a collective, universal, and impersonal nature, and the very real healing such work brings to people.

From these systems, invisible forms appear in our minds and guide our imagination, perception, and thinking. I have experienced in myself, and observed in others, how accessing these forms can help one to know the proper order in one's own life, and come to know the proper order of the universe. True happiness in this light can only be found by understanding the proper order of the universe, and by living in accordance with it. This means that we have to recognize the invisible background of reality, its importance in our lives, and accept the guidance that comes to us.

Jung's teaching is an incredible achievement because it can show us how we are connected with a non-empirical realm of the universe, in which we can find our life mission. Denying the transcendent aspects of our nature can lead to serious problems for our physical health and emotional wellbeing. Embracing them can lead to being who you REALLY are.

This book is written on the premise that the reader is able to accept that reality is not ONLY physical. If you need convincing, please take the time to read Tom Campbell's My Big TOE (Theory of Everything) trilogy for a comprehensive scientific argument from a trained physicist.

This book is not a dogmatic argument for a particular point of view. You do not have to accept any of the explanations to do the steps in the following chapters, or for them to work. This book is also not biographical in nature, but it does contain numerous examples from my own experience illustrating some of the points I will make.

The observable fact that every single life is heading towards non-physicality (death), can cause fear - or be inspiring. The promise of this book is that with a little effort and focus, your internal settings can be firmly and permanently affixed to the INSPIRE position.

Humanity started our path to global domination by smashing flint stones together to make tools. Now we are smashing atoms together in our search to find the penultimate elemental particle in order to make better tools. In other words, we are collectively still doing the same thing in the same way. It is high time we considered our individual life, our relationships and even our place in the world in a new light. It is time we turned the page. Please turn the page now.

Chapter One

QUESTIONS AND ANSWERS

First question: Why Do This?

Why do we do anything? The simple, physical, answer seems obvious, to live long and prosper. The Vulcans of Star Trek lore had it figured out. But they had the "advantage" of living without emotions. Why should anyone try to go from being physical to metaphysical? What does this even mean exactly? "Metaphysics" is the study of what philosophers call the "Ultimate Reality." It is classified as a branch of philosophy and is tasked with investigating the fundamental nature of being and the world that encompasses it. Metaphysics attempts to answer two basic questions about ultimate reality: What is there? What is it like?

Well, you don't have to be a professor of philosophy to have an opinion on these two questions. Most people are absolutely convinced that "ultimate reality" IS material reality and it feels like THIS. You know, slap the table - Bang! Solid, real! This book will lead you to another possibility of what the Ultimate Reality is and what it is like. It will not tell you what that is, and possibly no book can. However, whatever Ultimate Reality is, it is already happening to you right now. Perceiving it as purely physical and living life only for selfish, material reasons turns the natural flow of creation back on itself.

So, why do we do anything? Sure - live long, prosper, have children, or don't have children. But a purely material existence is not the purpose of human existence and everyone, on some level, probably already knows that. The fact that materialism is dominant today is not an accident. Most people come to accept a purely material reality after some thought and life experience. However, this is mainly due to where our attention has been focused. When attention is only directed outward, material reality is all you see.

Existentialist philosophy takes the idea of life as separation of individual beings from the material existence around them to its furthest logical conclusion. While I disagree with much of existential thought, the high value it places on the individual to live life "authentically" is admirable. However, this freedom to be authentic is found in existentialism to lead towards "angst" as the natural human state. The existential premise that existence is devoid of inherent meaning empowers humanity to create its own meaning while also dooming these efforts to ultimate failure.

Do you find the existential view of life fits yours? Do you agree the natural state of human life is, generally speaking, angst ridden in one way or another? Do you find your life devoid of meaning? Well, if you do, and you don't like that feeling, this book is for you! And being less anxious might be reason enough for "Why Do This?"

Second question: Who Is This Best For?

Anyone can do this. No strenuous exercise, no special diets, no confrontation, no workshops, and best of all, no homework. You will need to commit to meditating when you get to step four, but it should be easy and natural by then if you did steps one, two and three sincerely.

Some prior interest in the subject matter might make it easier to get the references in the book, but the steps are well explained with many real life examples, and laid out in a logical sequence so prior knowledge is not required. It is not "paint by numbers," but it IS only four steps and each step has only four main ideas that lead to the summary of that step. You need not have a lot of free time to work on the steps as they mainly call for internal consideration, and changes in attitude and how your attention is paid to things. I highly recommend this book for people who feel stressed out by their life.

Third question: What Am I Supposed To Do?

You are supposed to experience life as emanating from your own deepest level of being. These emanations should energize your life force, coalesce into your thoughts and dreams, and give power to your emotions. You are supposed to chart your path from the being level and manifest your uniqueness into your physical reality.

You are supposed to feel your being level emanations as intensely personal and familiar. You are supposed to be guided by an internal compass that gives course to your mental creativity and emotional authenticity. You are supposed to have integrity in your dealings with people and the material world. You are supposed to be who you REALLY are.

You ARE supposed to be here, now, reading this and committing yourself to taking the first step in changing your life.

Fourth question: Where Do I Start?

Like building anything, we start at the foundation. The human being is not purely physical, but the physical aspect is where we start. Before attention can be properly guided towards the less and less material aspects, the body has to be prepared so that it doesn't prevent us from focusing on more important things. This book will not prescribe particular diets, but hard facts about the impact of highly unhealthy eating on inner perception will be addressed. The goal here is not to lose weight or achieve a particular physical goal with the body. It is to change one's relationship with the body and put it in its proper place so we can move on to less substantial and better things.

Fifth question: When Is The Best Time To Do This?

In a word: Yesterday. The positive effects of coming to a proper understanding of the order of the universe have been life altering for me. However, I confess to taking many detours and rest stops on my own journey of recognition and awakening. So whenever you actually decide to take action, THAT is the best time, and when you take action, then and only then will the path open. But THIS is certainly the best time to read this book.

Sixth question: How Do I Do This?

We are going to do this systematically. In each step, examples from real case histories and from cultural references will guide your attention to the points that culminate in a summary statement of the step. Careful consideration and sincere reflection should lead to a personal experience of the statement as TRUE.

Step by step, you will replace things you believe with things you KNOW to be true. There will be suggested activities that should accelerate the process of change in how you view yourself and the world around you. Eventually your inner life experience should become quite different from one based on a materialistic worldview.

Chapter Two

THE FIRST STEP

You Are Not Your Body

You have a body. You are not only your body. These are compatible facts that do not contradict in any way. Envision it this way. The body is the shell of the egg. The emotions are the fluidic whites of the egg. The mind is the yolk of the egg. Your energy is the quickening, the fertilization of the egg. And the real you, the being level you, is what the egg is going to become. Seen this way, race, gender and much of what is held to be the bedrock of one's identity is merely the patterns and coloration on the shell. Some people like to be Easter eggs, but that has little to do with what the egg will hatch out to be.

In this metaphor, in our physical life, we can only access the shell of the egg directly. We can never physically access the emotional or intellectual worlds by material means. Breaking the shell will render the whole egg "done," and all you will have left is an empty shell and some emotions to clean up. It is a very sad thing for a "good egg" to go to waste before it has finished growing up all the way, however, if the egg was never fertilized to begin with - in this metaphor the person only used their emotional and intellectual aspects to fulfill material pursuits, it is much less sad because there wasn't going to be much of anything to "hatch" anyway.

Perhaps the strongest argument that human beings are not limited to the body is the testimony of people who have had near death experiences

(NDE's). There are literally thousands of books and accounts publicly available on this subject. Perhaps, someone you know has had one?

I will describe one account from someone in my own family. When one of my brothers was very young, he almost drowned. He stopped breathing for several minutes before he was revived and thankfully suffered no lasting effects. He did, however, retain a clear memory of the time when he was "dead."

According to my brother he remembers floating out of his body and immediately after leaving his body he is sent flying upwards toward the sky at an incredible speed. Suddenly arriving at a place he would later term "heaven" (he remembers it as filled with blissful emotion and beautiful lights), he instantly decides he wants to stay there. However, a voice that he would later call "God," which seems to be everywhere at once, firmly tells him that he can't stay and must go back. My brother resists, but finally asks for a gift in return. Instantly he is back in his body with a faint memory that his gift is to be able to tell when people are lying. Decades later, his memory of the incident is still crystal clear. I don't know if he can actually tell when people are lying, but he blames the fact that he finds it hard to be with people and has never married on this "gift."

For another powerful example, consider the case of Janine Shepard. Janine tells her story in the book "Defiant" which chronicles her remarkable life as an elite ski racer closing in on her bid to represent Australia in the Olympics. Suddenly her athletic career and almost her life were cut short by a speeding truck in a tragic accident. In the book, she recalls how during the ten days she hovered between life and death, faced with the difficult choice to let go or return to a body that would never be whole again, she found support from "another part of herself" that would not let her give up.

After six months in the hospital battling to rehabilitate permanent disabilities, she not only taught herself to walk again, something her doctors were doubtful of, but she found her passion again. In a moment of synchronicity, she sees a plane fly over her house at the precise moment she was ready to give up on life, and she knew she would fly. Despite the misgivings of her flight instructors, Janine eventually earned her wings as both a pilot and later as an aerobatics instructor. Her TED talk, available on YouTube, is called "You Are Not Your Body."

Or consider the case of Martin Pistorius, born in Johannesburg, South Africa in 1975. At the age of twelve an unknown illness left him wheelchair bound and unable to speak. First he lost his voice and stopped eating on his own then he slept constantly and shunned human contact. Doctors were mystified. Within eighteen months he was mute and wheelchair-bound. Martin's parents were told an unknown degenerative disease had left him with the mind of a baby and less than two years to live.

Martin was moved to care centers for severely disabled children where he spent the next fourteen years. The stress and heartache destroyed his parents' marriage and shook the entire family to the core. Martin was gone. Or so they thought.

In fact, Martin's emotional and intellectual capacities never dimmed. It was only his ability to communicate through his body that had been affected. He was able to fully perceive the breakdown of the people around him, and there to hear his mother tell him it would have been better if he had died. Incredibly, Martin had been misdiagnosed and only the eventual intervention of a conscientious nurse salvaged his destiny. Martin survived these years of unimaginable horror and lived to meet the "love of his life," and to tell his story to the world in the New York Times bestseller, "Ghost Boy."

The book tells his heart-wrenching story as Martin shares his memories of the consequences of the misdiagnosis. It also shows how the failure of his physical aspect actually fueled the unthinkable endurance of his mental and emotional aspects, and led to his ultimate emergence from darkness.

Fortunate or unfortunate, depending on what extreme experiences like these lead to, and how one reacts and interprets them, most of us are spared from having them. However, we all have to contend with the fact that our body is very much mortal. A body-identified person living in a material world is a pretty fragile being. Most of us learn at a young age that everybody is going to die eventually. This realization is often a deeply affecting one that causes people to make deep, long lasting decisions about the meaning of life that they rarely consciously consider again.

What is often confusing is that despite the surface confession of belief in this or that most people have mixed feelings about death and are struggling with what they really think. So they latch onto whatever is at hand and commit to it. Most adults are like that and their kids learn to be the same. For those who already profess a firm faith in the continuation of the spirit after bodily death, I urge you to go deeper and seek to manifest more of that spirit while you still have a body.

In these materialistic times, it is not surprising that body modification, gender reassignment, plastic surgeries of various degrees and powerful makeup technologies (they are expensive enough to call it tech) are popular. If you can't feel better by doing something internal then do something external. If you are only body-identified, the only way to feel pleasure is physically.

Consider the intense feelings that drive transgender people. The gender reassignment procedure is invasive and arduous – certainly not to be taken lightly. Not to mention very costly. However, the relief that people claim to receive seems heartfelt.

PERSONAL INTERLUDE – Beijing, China, September of 1998.

I have been assigned to the American Embassy in Beijing as the contracting officer. It is a huge operation spread out in a large number of buildings all over the city. Through some friends in LA, I got to know a Chinese-American record producer who relocated to China early and had signed most of the up and coming singers, and now they were big stars. The music market in China had blown up in the years after he moved there, and now HE was famous in the industry.

I was invited to his birthday party and expected to breeze in and out like most of the diplomatic functions I had to attend. It turns out this was going to be a much more interesting kind of evening. I find myself seated next to Ms. X at a huge round table with 50 or so local celebrities.

Ms. X was famous as a dancer, but her real fame was being one of China's first transgendered people (so I was told). As most everyone proceed to get very drunk, and some to go throw up and return to drink more, I am reminded of the vomitadero ("barfatoriums") of ancient Rome. Ms. X stays sober, as do I. We have a good conversation which convinced me that her gender reassignment was her authentic choice.

Not feeling right in one's body is hardly limited to gender. When I was sure I would not get any taller, I still wanted to be a little taller. However, when I saw the lengths to which some people were willing to go, (you guessed it, leg extending surgery) I learned to be comfortable just as I am. As I got older, many people around me started to get cosmetic surgery. Most are happy with the results, but more than a few fell into the "one more, to fix the last one" trap.

My point is this, something that seems to work and makes one feel better, might not be the best or lasting fix for what is "wrong." From my encounter with Ms. X and other people facing similar issues, I find the alteration they seek is an attempt to meet an external image that will make them feel better rather than an inner image. This is only my impression, but it is consistent with my idea that if one can conform to an inner image and be comfortable, no external alteration would be required.

If someone is overly identified with the body, it is easy to become preoccupied with how others look at one's body. When someone becomes focused on how one is judge based on their outward appearance eventually that person will start judge him or herself in the same way that others do.

Your Body Is What You Eat

Every cell in your body is replaced many times over during your lifetime. Even the hard skeletal cells only last a few years and then are dissolved and regrown. Not long ago, it was thought that what guided the body's amazing ability to build and repair itself was DNA, and that chemical and molecular mechanisms were behind it all. However, with the stem cell revolution and discoveries by pioneers like Dr. Bruce Lipton, these ideas have had to change. In his book "Biology of Belief," Dr. Lipton clearly shows that attitude, mindset, and belief send orders to the cells and alter their activity.

To help those not familiar with stem cell technology and Dr. Lipton's contributions, you should know that he is an internationally recognized leader in bridging science and spirit. He received his Ph.D. from the University of Virginia at Charlottesville before joining the Department of Anatomy at the University of Wisconsin's School of Medicine in 1973. In 1982, Dr. Lipton began examining the principles of quantum physics and how they might be integrated into his understanding of the cell's information processing systems.

His research at Stanford University's School of Medicine revealed to him that the environment, operating though the cell membrane, controlled the behavior and physiology of the cell, turning genes on and off. Dr. Lipton's novel scientific approach transformed his personal life as well. His work led him to a deeper understanding of cell biology and through examining the non-physical mechanisms by which the mind controls the body he arrived at the existence of an immortal spirit.

He applied his science to his personal biology, and as he tells it in his book, his external well-being improved as he changed his inner view of life. Eventually, the quality and character of his daily life was greatly enhanced.

The implications of Dr. Lipton's research and personal experiences strongly support the overall thesis that reality flows from non-physical into the physical. However, a much more direct effect on your body than the subtle, nonetheless very powerful, forces Lipton writes about, is your conscious decision of what to eat and even more vitally HOW MUCH to eat.

Biologists have proven that caloric restriction will increase the lifespan of every species that experiences it. Above a certain minimum, caloric restriction brings on increased cellular repair, better metabolic regulation, and improved immune response. The answer is obvious. Running lean is good for you. Clogging up the engine with too much fuel is a very bad idea. But the kind of over-eating prevalent today is akin to filling your car's gas tank then soaking up the seat cushions too. Eating too much is the epidemic of our time even as endemic hunger still stalks society's underclass.

Recent studies and news reports on caloric restriction makes clear the link between cutting down the amount you eat and helping you live longer. A study by the National Institute on Aging, a division of the US Department of Health, suggests that fewer calories in your diet as an adult can lead to a longer and healthier life. However, it is important to note that the research is showing that cutting the amount of food at a younger age was not found to be beneficial.

The researchers found that cutting calories dials back illness related to the so-called metabolic syndrome in older adults. They found adult monkeys who received 30 percent less food tended to live up to two years longer for males and almost six years longer in females. If similar results could be seen in humans, it could extend people's lives for up to 18 years. But, the researchers cautioned that in the real world the effect would likely be less as other aspects of lifestyle would have an impact on how long a person could live.

Speaking as someone whose father died from complications related to diabetes, whose mother and brother are diabetic, I have witnessed how difficult it is to control the craving to overeat even when the dangers and the eventualities are well known. I have observed how intelligent people are unable to control their eating habits simply through knowledge of the ill effect and using their will power. It appears to me that their failure to protect their health by controlling their food intake was not necessarily a lack of rectitude, but rather a habitual overdependence on something material - food - to fulfill non-physical needs (like love).

Once bad eating habits are set, and eventually, illness takes hold, it becomes ever harder to change the behaviors that are the cause of the problem. As permanent changes happen within the body and also in the psychology of the person, it becomes almost impossible to change course. Insulin is the treatment for diabetes, but it is not a cure. The cure, eating less food of a more healthy variety, is as obvious as it seems to be impossible for most sufferers.

PERSONAL INTERLUDE: Tokyo, Japan, May of 1993.

I am working at the American Embassy in Tokyo. It is my first REAL overseas assignment as a diplomat after having to "resign" to serve at the American Institute in Taiwan on my first tour. It is a great city. I have a prestigious posting in the Economic Section. It is well compensated work that I like and in my personal life, I am dating a beautiful South Korean woman born in Japan, and we are starting to get serious. I am feeling on top of the world...

Then one night, late, sometime after midnight, the phone rings. Must be work, another "night action immediate" cable from Washington...

"Hello?"

"Michael, mom... your dad, he's not going to make it."

"What... What??"

"His blood pressure, he got a stroke. He's not going to wake up... We are going to pull the plug."

"No. Don't do that. Don't do anything until I get there!"

"You better hurry..."

When the doctor reviewed my dad's situation at the "family meeting" to decide if we would keep him on life support, it became clear that he had been in the danger zone for quite a long time before the stroke. His eating habits were way too sugary and he probably didn't have the right medicine. You would think seeing him go like that would have been a warning to the rest of his family. However, following his death, my mom went on to develop full-blown diabetes. My brother had pancreatitis and then full-blown diabetes. And I "suffered" several more years of "entertainment" dining (I could claim occupational hazard for some of it) before I got a doctor's warning on my cholesterol levels.

However, a major change in attitude towards eating and maintaining a balanced, sustainable diet only came years later after I decided to try changing the way I eat for an internal, intellectual reason. For me, all the physical motivations of a better body, good health, etc. didn't do it. Because emotionally, I was still committed to the eating habits that I had built up. Ultimately, it was intellectual curiosity that did it for me.

I had developed a strong curiosity in wanting to replicate some of the caloric restriction experiments and see the effects for myself. That was what finally got me to change how and what I ate. I really wanted to know what caloric restriction would do, and the only way to know was to do it myself. So, the reason for the change came from the intellectual aspect that overrode the emotional ties that was holding my eating behavior to what it was.

Reading about how little I should eat to replicate even some of the more moderate experiments was cause for pause. But there is only one way to know how something feels, and that is to do it yourself. The first few days were very hard. Hunger pangs are the most urgent part of the desire for food, but it was the constant mental debate about continuing or not that took the most effort. After a few days, I came up with a way to hold on during the few moments of actual pain that comes after the growling stomach and the hunger pangs peak.

Physically, what I did was hug my belly and think about all the great physical effects of what I was enduring. Emotionally, I let myself feel proud of my ability to overcome this final obstacle before I could reward myself with some food. I literally "embraced my hunger." Intellectually, I made hunger a tool that I was using. Then I ate a little.

Past the halfway point, things got a lot easier. My body adjusted to this new routine. The feelings of hunger got less intense and the desire to eat became much tamer. At the end of my experimental period of 10 days, the result was remarkable and undeniable. I had completely reset my eating habits. I lost some weight, but I was not overweight to begin with. What I learned was that I could control my desire for food. What I continue to do now is comfortably eat less than half of the amount I was eating before and still feel more energetic.

WARNING: Caloric restriction might not be suitable for everyone. Please consult a medical professional if you decide to try this yourself.

The old Chinese peasants had a saying, "For commoners to eat is the ultimate heaven." I can see given the harshness of their lives, why they would not find much else to be happy about, but it's a very limited happiness. There is an "ancient Chinese secret" to maximize the happiness one gets from eating. And the secret is this: <u>quality over quantity</u>. The best result of my experience with caloric restriction is that I pay much more attention now to eating GOOD food. Since I now limit my total intake of food, it is easier to just fill the shopping basket with a few quality items.

Junk food is now out. MSG is assiduously avoided. Even meat is now just an occasional happening.

For someone who got through college on instant noodles and spam, and used to feast on a whole rack of BBQ ribs, it's a pretty dramatic change.

Overall, the purpose of this book is to help people bring their physical attention, emotional perceptions, and intellectual power from being outwardly directed to get something to being inwardly directed to "get it." As the most dense and physical aspect of you, your body has the ability to be more or less "dense" within its range of existence. Overeating leading to obesity and all of the attendant health issues that arise will get in the way of any effort to remove one's attention from purely material reality. You can't look past the physical if you are mainly looking at how to eat it.

Eating should be pleasurable. It is required to sustain physical life, but it needs to remain in its proper province. It belongs in the lowest aspect of human experience. You can never fulfill needs arising from the higher aspects by doing MORE of something that gives you pleasure but only in the context of physical fulfillment. While eating too much, or eating junk food, will definitely cause harm to you physically, its harmful effects also extend past that.

While it is very possible to develop strong emotional and intellectual aspects of the consciousness with a less than athletic body, one's ability to access the energetic and being levels will be deeply impacted. A body that is not at ease is near disease. A body that is in a unpleasant state demands your attention, and it will get it with pain. A body in such a state WILL get in the way of the level of introspection and directed attention that will be required as we proceed. There is no way to sugar coat this bitter pill.

However, we are NOT talking about some external standard of fitness from outside. The correct amount of fitness for your body should be arrived at from within. How pleasant do you need to feel so that your body does not get in the way? And having a body that gets in the way does not mean NO WAY. To arrive at what is the best diet for you, you should consult the body itself. You need to look… within.

Your Body Is A Democracy

Every cell in your body is a reflection of the whole body. The body has organs, the cell has organelles. The body has a respiratory system, a vascular system, etc. and so does the cell. By "your body is a democracy," what is meant is to use the political system as a metaphor for understanding that the body is not one thing. Most people today actually suffer from a psychological condition of dissociation from internal feedback.

There are some diseases that humans suffer that can never happen to animals as they lack the capacity to suffer from the cause of the behavior that leads up to the disease. Put another way, geese would never make their livers into pate given a choice, and that is why humans have to force feed them to make "foie gras." However, more than a few humans give themselves the same condition without being forced. One must surmise that on the way to drinking oneself into liver failure, the liver was not consulted on the matter.

Dissociation from the body can be a part of, and even a cause of, other psychological issues. In itself, the condition is particularly harmful to reaching deeper levels of perception leading to a glimpse of the Ultimate Reality. Think of it this way, you want a sound foundation for your skyscraper? You have to start with deep enough pylons (see "Leaning Tower of San Francisco"). The condition can also be seen as the "building the second floor before the first" syndrome. It is imperative that the body be in a good working order before trying to resolve higher echelon issues.

You are not your body, but it is the only thing you have to carry you around here. If you are stuck in your car and can never get out of it for your entire life, how would you treat it? You would probably learn every meter, try every control, and use it as best as you possibly could. Treating your body the same way - learning every signal, gauging every impulse and trying various fuel blends to make it work at its best - is the same idea.

Your body is like a democracy in another way, it works best when it works together. Next time you are tempted to eat or drink excessively, think of your poor stomach! Your body actually comes with a life time guarantee for free repairs and upgrades, but wrong usage voids the warranty.

Balance And Sustainability

Once you try enough diets and other people's advice, try really listening to your own body. Eating can become something you won't have to track or fret over too much. Everything the body requires has a balance point; not too much, not too little. Pregnant women are famous for developing "strange" appetites due to changes in their bodies. They seem to know they want "this" because their body lacks "that." Everyone is a little like that. It's a subtle feeling, but the body does transmit "up" signals into conscious awareness.

I am NOT saying eat like a pregnant woman!

Eat less, eat well, and eat what you feel like once you establish good communication with your body. But don't just do that. As Bruce Lipton has shown in his work, the body clearly conforms to the prevailing emotional attitudes one holds towards (and subconscious view as well) it, and the world that it lives in.

The process that this book is about starts with a good physical foundation. You need to take good care of your body because once you adjust to an inner-directed life things are going to get much better, and you want to stick around for that. Balance and sustainability go hand in hand.

The Body Knowing

Ever have a "gut feeling?" This phenomenon is so common it has its own name. I have had many such feelings and most were very accurate. The onset of a gut feeling serves to alert me to pay attention to some detail that I might have missed otherwise. When I ignored the feeling, I usually regret it later.

Scientists have found that neural (brain) tissue exists in the heart as well as the bowels. As Michael Gershon, M.D., explains in his book "The Second Brain", the independent network of over 100 billion neurons in the gut is vital to our health. Not only does this "second brain" send and receive signals to and from the "main" brain, it can cause illness, all by itself, if it is over stressed.

According to Gershon, the feeling of "butterflies in the stomach" arises when the brain sends a message of anxiety to the gut, which then sends messages back to the brain that it's "unhappy" as well. Aside from this purely physical explanation, I would assign even greater significance to this type of feeling than just neurons talking to each other. It certainly "feels" like it is more to me. I would argue that this is indicative of a junction of the physical and emotional aspects of a human being. For anyone who has ever felt it very strongly in themselves, I think they would agree.

Perhaps there are even intersections of the material world and the emotional world. You might think that these feelings that seem to connect to events are just coincidences, but Jung's concept of "synchronicity" certainly goes beyond what is implied in coincidence. For Jung, synchronicity is not just things happening at the same time, co-incidental in time, rather that they are timed, "synchronized," to happen together to transmit an emotional message...

PERSONAL INTERLUDE: *Enping Village / Zhuhai SEZ (Special Economic Zone), China, March of 1999.*

Right after my dad died, I start getting dreams with him in it. They all have a "different" quality to them, but I just figured it was me wanting them to be that way. Then my mom and one of my brothers both said they had dreams indicating my dad didn't want his ashes sitting in a dusty guestroom anymore and we should arrange to bury "him" back in the ancestral village.

Well, as luck would have it, my uncle on my mom's side still had a lot of friends back in the village, and he was able to help us make it happen. I was working in Hong Kong at the time which turned out to be the perfect logistical base for this "international" operation.

It eventually turns into a cast of thousands, well at least hundreds, as people come from the surrounding villages to get the "lucky money" being handed out as part of the tradition for the returnees from the "Gold Mountain" (America) when they bring "the fallen leaf back to the roots."

The whole thing still seems like a dream...

When it's all over and we're almost ready to drive to Zhuhai to take the ferry back to Hong Kong, my mom somehow gets an appointment with a "famous" local soothsayer. I go with her and we are ushered into the presence of a very average looking Chinese peasant woman. As I am sitting in her newspaper and pinup calendar wall-papered house, she starts to tell my mom stuff about our house in San Francisco, her personal life, and her childhood. Some of it actually does get pretty close, but it's nothing she couldn't find out by asking around or just guessing. A pretty decent mentalist is what I am thinking...

I ask her, "what about me?"

"You are like the noonday sun now. There is nothing you want to know from me."

Wow, she IS psychic!

They ramble on... I miss some of it as the local dialect is not what I am used to. Then near the end, she says to my mom, "And he WILL come to you as a butterfly to show you he is happy with the burial ceremony you performed. It was a good showing for everyone."

Yeah, right...

My mom, however, is excited and starts telling everyone what the "mo-por" (witch lady) said. It was so cute watching my sister translate to her little girl that grandpa is going to turn into a butterfly and come see us!

As we get into Zhuhai, I am driving the lead car and going slow so the car behind won't get lost on the way to the hotel I booked. Out of the corner of my eye, I notice a... butterfly. Is it... following the car? I turn towards the hotel and keep an eye of the thing. It IS still following me...

I lose sight of it as I focus on parking the car. We get everyone together and start walking in when my niece yells, "Look, its grandpa!"

Before I can react, people behind me start yelling, "Don't move!"

I stop in my tracks, but instinctively turn my head to see what is going on. As I do, I see the butterfly on my shoulder. I can tell that it is the same one that was following the car.

Before I could do anything else, my mom walks up and picks the butterfly off my shoulder and puts it on hers. "Take a picture," she tells my sister.

My sister fumbles for her camera and manages to take a couple of shots.

"Poor thing," I think to myself, "must be sick or disoriented or something."

As I have this thought, the butterfly shoots up in the air and in less than 10 seconds it has flown out of sight.

"Well, I guess it wasn't sick…"

So how does reality have this ability to synchronize physical events and emotional meaning? Actually, it is all energy (information, if you really get down to it), but let's save that for a bit later. For now, let's look at more evidence that indicates reality isn't the same old physical material reality (PMR) that we are used to.

The concept of teleportation comes primarily from science fiction literature, but developments in quantum theory and general relativity physics means numerous teleportation breakthroughs have been made. One example is the work being done at the University of Innsbruck where they successfully teleported single atoms (the work was published in the journal Nature). They were able to teleport in the form of transferring quantum states between two atoms including the atom's energy, motion, magnetic field and other physical properties.

Another study by scientists at the University of Queensland in 2013 demonstrated that successful teleportation could be done with solid state systems. This is another process by which quantum information is transmitted from one place to another without sending a physical carrier of information, and is made possible through the phenomenon of entanglement. This level of quantum teleportation has since been replicated by numerous scientists all over the world many times now.

In 2014 an article in Collective Evolution (next to a photo of the Star Trek away team half dematerialized) teased readers with this headline, "SCIENTISTS REPORT TELEPORTATION OF PHYSICAL OBJECTS FROM ONE LOCATION TO ANOTHER." At first, I thought, a bit sensationalized, but AFTER I read it, I thought not nearly sensational enough. Here are the salient points for your consideration.

The article was a review of papers published in China about "psychic conveyance" or teleportation facilitated by human consciousness. The article quotes Eric Davis, Ph.D. of the Foreign Broadcast Information Service (FBIS) on how he learned about psychic conveyance. According to the article, Davis claims that, "it became known to me, along with several colleagues both inside and outside of government, that anomalous teleportation has been scientifically investigated and separately documented by the Department of Defense."

Davis also says that as part of his work at FBIS, he reviewed papers published in the People's Republic of China (PRC) in the 1980s that reported on "Experiments on the Transfer of Objects Performed by Unusual Abilities of the Human Body." The papers claimed that "gifted children" were able to cause the teleportation of small, physical objects from one place to another. The objects included watches, horseflies, other insects, radio micro-transmitters, photosensitive paper and more.

According to the papers reviewed by Davis, the participants never touched the objects beforehand. The experiments were done under both blind and double-blind conditions, and the researchers involved came from reputable colleges and sectors of the Defense Ministry. The papers were reportedly prepared because it was deemed necessary that unclassified versions of the test results be released for wider academic viewing to facilitate research into the extraordinary results.

More research was reportedly done by the Aerospace Medicine Engineering Institute in Beijing in 1990. This study reported several experiments involving high speed video capture of the transfer of test specimens like nuts, matches, nails, pills and other items through sealed paper envelopes, sealed glass bottles and tubes, sealed plastic film canisters and other denser types of barriers without the containers being breached. All of these experiments reported using "gifted" children and adults who could teleport the objects.

The reports claim that in frame by frame viewing, the test specimens could be seen "winking out" and reappearing outside their enclosure.

The specimens are show to have remained in their original state after teleportation including showing the insects still alive.

According to Davis, the Chinese papers are extremely well written with many photographs and schematic diagrams of the various experimental setups. The experimental protocols were explained in lengthy detail and thorough data and statistical analysis were presented in the results.

These reports showed that different Chinese research groups designed different experimental methods using "gifted psychics" and were able to independently replicate similar results of teleporting test specimens through various barriers. Video recorded some of the test specimens melding or blending with the walls of sealed containers, and then simply disappear from inside the container only to reappear at another location.

Radio Micro-transmitters used as test specimens changed in frequency dramatically during teleportation and the researchers concluded that this indicated that the transmitter was in an altered physical state during teleportation. The frequency of the transmission remained the same before and after teleportation.

The papers stressed that the experiments were conducted under conditions where the chance of fraud and sleight of hand was eliminated, and multiple outside witnesses (including military and intelligence experts) were present at all times. The scientists conducting the tests could not offer any explanation for the results based on "known science."

Commenting on the Chinese papers, Davis is positive that they are genuine. Asked to surmise on what was happening in the experiments, Davis says, "it is necessary to invoke a new physics, which somehow unifies human consciousness with quantum and space-time physics, in order to understand psychic teleportation and related PK phenomena. The results of the Chinese Teleportation experiments can be explained as a human consciousness phenomenon."

Davis further speculates that the gifted children and others, "somehow acts to move or rotate test specimens through another dimension so that specimens are able to penetrate the solid barriers of their containers without physically breaching them."

So... does Eric Davis, Ph.D. from FBIS (whatever that is) know what he is talking about? Is his statement that people inside the US government knows that "anomalous teleportation" has been scientifically investigated and has been documented by the Department of Defense to be believed?

Due to a pledge to the person who gave me the information not to disclose certain details in public, I can only say I have good reasons to believe the Chinese experiments described in the papers reviewed by Davis did take place and the results were accurately reported.

As for Dr. Davis, his public profile is well known in scientific circles. A quick search will reveal that Dr. Eric W. Davis received his Ph.D. in astrophysics from the University of Arizona in 1991. His fields of specialization include spacecraft exploration of the outer solar system, planetary sciences, relativity theory and cosmology, space mission engineering, and NASA Breakthrough Propulsion Physics.

Besides working for FBIS, he is also a research physicist at the Institute for Advanced Studies in Austin, Texas, and as well as being the CEO of Warp Drive Metrics. During 1996–2002 he was with the National Institute for Discovery Science in Las Vegas, NV where he served as the staff Aerospace/Astrophysics researcher. He also participated in the NASA Breakthrough Propulsion Physics program, and co-founded the Advanced Deep Space Transport Technology Assessment Group at NASA-JSC.

In 1995 he joined the sciences-mathematics faculty at the University of Maryland Asian Division where he was stationed at the 8th Fighter Wing in Kunsan, South Korea. While in Kunsan, he developed Air Force sponsored space mission engineering and Korean theater space reconnaissance training.

Dr. Eric Davis is a recognized expert on the quantum vacuum, zero point energy, traversable wormholes, trans-warp drive and antimatter propulsion. He has also been recognized by the American Institute of Aeronautics and Astronautics for outstanding contributions to national defense and space public policy.

Based on his resume alone, we can surmise that he knows more than the average person on the subject being discussed in the article.

Oh, and FBIS? Well, that would be the Foreign Broadcast Information Service, the intelligence component of the Central Intelligence Agency's (CIA) Directorate of Science and Technology. It monitors, translates, and disseminates within the U.S. government news and information from media sources outside the United States. Its headquarters is in Reston, Virginia, and it maintains over 20 monitoring stations worldwide.

In November 2005, its name was changed to the Open Source Center. Its declared mandate is to continue collecting and analyzing publicly available intelligence for the CIA and distribute that to relevant parties in the U.S. government.

One of the collection centers "Open Source" maintains is in Hong Kong. I was buddies with the director of that center while I worked at the Consulate-General. We use to go on long treks over in Zhuhai on weekends and talk religion. Very nice guy! He was a Quaker who knew about the Baha'i Faith, but for some reason kept calling it "Bahaism." I have pictures of us somewhere… Those were fun times… Now I feel nostalgic and… hungry?

See how emotions can creep up on your body? I was just transported back to the super meals we used to get for next to nothing at a tiny seaside restaurant off the side of the road next to the Zhuhai International School.

This is a good point to introduce the next step in our process, "You Are Not Your Emotions." Emotions are so closely related to the physical body that many people feel them in the body or as a physical thing, especially when their intensity is very high. Depression has a color, grey. Anger has a temperature, heat. But what are emotions and where do they come from?

Chapter Three

THE SECOND STEP

You Are Not Your Emotions

You are not your emotions. If you really think about it, you do not even "have" emotions. You can't buy one, you can't rent one, and you can't own one. You can only feel them. You experience them. You can try to hold on to them and maintain the feeling through will, mental effort (like holding a grudge), but it takes continual effort. Memories or fantasies can evoke emotions, but they are sure to feel manufactured, artificial. Genuine emotions ARISE within you. They wash over you, they envelop you, and they can even overwhelm you.

PERSONAL INTERLUDE: Taipei, Taiwan, November 2nd, 2000.

On Halloween, 23:17 Taipei local time, Singapore Airlines flight 006 attempts to take off from the wrong runway at Chiang Kai-shek International Airport during a typhoon. The aircraft crashes into construction equipment on the runway and bursts into flames, killing 83 of the 179 occupants aboard. Many are Americans and I am sent from the Consulate in Hong Kong to help the overwhelmed staff in Taipei to provide assistance to American citizen survivors and the families of the dead. With the storm still dissipating, not all the bodies have been identified. On the second day after my arrival, I am helping a Chinese-American man who doesn't speak Mandarin very well to fill out his paperwork and notice that we are the same age.

Both of his parents are listed as missing, but we both know there is little hope, as all the survivors had already been located. As we are working through the little pile of forms, a local official asks me to tell him they think they found his mother and need him to identify the body. He asks if I could go with him and I agree. As we walk into the hanger that serves as the makeshift morgue, I suddenly smell bad BBQ – the combined scent of too much lighter fluid and burnt meat.

A split second later, my mind accurately interprets what the smell is... then we see the body. It is completely blackened with no way to tell if it is a man or a woman at first glance. My companion collapses onto the floor, weeping. I try to say something but when he glances up at me, I am speechless.

His face is the picture of inconsolable.

Rocks vibrate. Plants vibrate and grow and reproduce. Animals do all that with movement and feeling. As far as we can tell, until they started living with humans, animals did not need therapy or "whispering" to. Humans, on the other hand, seem to have had emotional problems since a very long time ago. In the Old Testament, it is recorded that Cain killed his brother Able because he was jealous of Jehovah's favor towards Able. Helen of Troy is supposed to have launched an invasion fleet of a thousand ships because she ran off with a younger man.

Lust, passion, ambition, betrayal, revenge! Where would world history (and kungfu movies) be without them? But a human being cannot BE any or all of these emotions. By their nature, emotions communicate something; they are fleeting and they carry a message.

Animals do very well with their emotions because they don't hold onto them the way humans do. Holding on to the memory of an emotion and identifying with it is (I'm sorry to say) kind of ridiculous. But it is ALL TOO COMMON. Someone who is passive-aggressive is over-identified with an emotional attitude. They might even say, "I AM stubborn." It is common in English to refer to emotions as being them. "I am happy." "I am sad." You say you HAVE a body, but you say you ARE your feelings, because emotions come from a higher aspect of being human than physical sensations.

The reason it is so easy to over-identify with your emotions is they bring feelings so intense that they can go beyond the body's physical sensation. However, no matter how much one is swept away by an emotion, one is still able to feel the body, and sometimes the body is even more sensitized by a strong emotion. Emotion is often felt as being *in* the body and in extreme circumstances it is sensed as a tangible thing.

Some people fear emotional intimacy precisely due to the intensity and vulnerability it elicits. However, it would be a mistake to let fear, an emotion itself, prevent one from exploring the depth and breadth of one's emotional aspect. Emotions connect us to our source, both figuratively and literally. They allow us to feel empathy for our animal cousins and to be more deeply connected to the Earth. In his books on discovering Binaural Sound Technology and how experimenting with them on himself led to him having numerous out of body experiences (OBE's), Robert Monroe writes movingly about the many trials and errors that he experienced in his "astral travels" to discover the "Missing Basic" that would help him move farther in his journeys.

SPOILER ALERT

Don't read the next line if you have not read Bob's trilogy and you want to find out what this Missing Basic is for yourself.

The Missing Basic: A deep emotional connection to the planet.

I want to pause here to pay tribute to Bob Monroe. In my own journey inwards to deeper aspects of my being, discovering Bob's books were incredibly helpful. I strongly recommend you read all three of his books if you have not had the pleasure. Bob lived an open and public life, and he wrote about his unusual experiences and shared them as widely as he could. Here are some interesting facts of his early life and some specifics from his work with OBE's.

Robert Allan Monroe was born in Indiana weighing some twelve pounds. He grew up in Lexington, Kentucky, and Columbus, Ohio. According to his third book Ultimate Journey, he dropped out of Ohio

State University in his sophomore year due to a hospital stay for a facial burn that caused him to fall behind in his studies. During almost a year away from college, a desire to find work led him to become a hobo who rode freight trains. He returned to Ohio State to graduate after having studied pre-med, English, engineering, and journalism.

In 1953, Bob Monroe formed RAM Enterprises, a corporation that produced network radio programs, as many as 28 programs monthly, principally dramatic and popular quiz shows. In 1956 his firm created a Research and Development division to study the effects of various sound patterns on human consciousness, including the sleep state. Monroe was especially interested in the concept of "sleep-learning" and this seemed a natural direction to take, applying audio production methods used in the firm's commercial activity to this new field. His purpose was to find more constructive uses for this new technology, and the results of this research have become internationally known.

According to his own account, while experimenting with sleep-learning in 1958, he experienced an unusual phenomenon, which he described as sensations of paralysis and vibration accompanied by a bright light that appeared to be shining on him from a shallow angle. Bob reported that this occurred another nine times over the next six weeks, culminating in his first out-of-body experience (OBE).

He recorded his initial account in the 1971 book *Journeys Out of the Body* and went on to become a prominent researcher in the field of human consciousness. Bob later authored two more books on his OBEs, *Far Journeys* in 1985 and shortly before his death he published *Ultimate Journey* in 1994.

The Monroe Institute (TMI) is a nonprofit education and research organization, devoted to the exploration of human consciousness founded by Robert Monroe after he started having OBEs. One of its core activities is teaching techniques based on audio-guidance processes to expand consciousness and explore areas of consciousness not normally available in the waking state. The Institute has an Outreach program, where accredited facilitators travel to various locations around the world and deliver workshops. Robert Monroe died on March 17, 1995, at the age of 79.

Thank you, Mr. Monroe, for the work you did to rediscover what the ancients referred to as astral travel for our modern times. I am convinced that very soon, people will appreciate the scientific approach you brought to this spiritual subject as more and more of us comes to accept that we are more than a material being. Your books helped me at the time I needed that help the most.

The Water Of Life The Fire Of Life

Emotions connect the intellectual aspect to the physical aspect. As the second most "substantial" part of the human being, emotions convey messages from the intellect to the body. Something happens, you react with an emotion because you THINK this has happened, but then you realize you were mistaken and the emotion disappears or changes to the correct one that corresponds to the situation. Someone who is overly identified with their emotions to an extreme degree will find it hard to let go of an emotion despite a change in understanding because they have the problem of thinking they ARE their emotions.

Someone who feels slighted then realizes no insult was meant, but retaliates anyway is, by definition, emotionally disturbed. Someone who actively manipulates or harasses others for their own emotional "pleasure" is most likely full of fear and devoted only to their own emotional sense of self. If this reaches an extreme level, you will see sociopathic tendencies.

Healthy emotions are given their meaning through thoughtful deliberation.

PERSONAL INTERLUDE: San Francisco, June of 2012.

I am waiting for a bus, minding my own business. Three touristy looking Chinese, a man and two women, are speaking in Mandarin and a huge black guy around 6'8" has his back to them and is reading a paperback book. The man is gesticulating and talking, I tune out. He pauses, and then he says, "nigger nigger nigger…"

My attention is suddenly focused on the black guy as he turns with an angry scowl. He realizes that the man is speaking in a foreign language and all three are paying him no attention, then he looks at me. I freeze my face. Slowly looking away... Nothing to see here... He turns back to his book. Then it dawns on me! "Ne ge, ne ge, ne ge..." He was saying "that that that..." in Mandarin and trying to think of something.

Emotions make us feel alive viscerally (perhaps it has something to do with all that brain tissue in the gut). Good or bad they are a part of your life that is going to be with you. You can't sock away your emotions no matter how hard you try. As any Star Trek fan can tell you, even Vulcans have to deal with the "Pon Farr" (Amok Time)!

So what do you do with them? Why, nothing, of course!

What do you do with a message you have read? Delete it? Forget about it? To dwell on emotion is to give them power that they do not deserve. You should reflect on them to make sure you have the correct understanding of the situation that the emotion is drawing you to before you punch somebody in the face.

Emotions are not good or bad. They are purely situational, like water and fire. The right amount in the right place, your life is great. The wrong one in the wrong way, you get hate (or chaos). To react with anger to an angry person is precisely what "fighting fire with fire" implies. Perhaps in the physical world there are instances where that is the right thing to do. In the emotional life such a tactic only benefits divorce lawyers.

You always fight "fire" with "water" in the emotional life. If you feed a feeling of anger with self-justifying thoughts that bend the facts in your favor, you will enrage yourself. If you yell at a person you find annoying before understanding their situation, you are asking for trouble.

Often, a negative emotional response is triggered by our own internal fear or underlying issue. A person who feels inadequate will be very sensitive to anything that triggers their fear of failure. Getting rid of one's own fears is the best way to avoid emotionally blowing things out of proportion. Having "a chip on your shoulder" is exactly the type of behavior that reveals an overabundance of internal fear. Even if someone is insulting you or being annoying, that behavior is about THEIR emotional state. The person you find most annoying is actually the person who is able to help you most in this regard. Instead of focusing on WHAT is annoying you, look within for WHY it is annoying.

A person full of internal fear is like an unkempt ammunition dump. One spark and... BLAM!

Abdu'l-Bahá wisely taught that, *"When a thought of war comes, oppose it by a stronger thought of peace. A thought of hatred must be destroyed by a more powerful thought of love. Thoughts of war bring destruction to all harmony, well-being, restfulness and content. Thoughts of love are constructive of brotherhood, peace, friendship, and happiness."*

Not everyone is equally capable in physical or intellectual ways, but in terms of being capable of learning to direct one's emotional energies per the above quote, we are ALL equally capable once we learn to pay attention.

Directed properly from a mind that seeks to understand the truth in a situation, emotions are the best guides an intellect can have. Materialistic, self-centered minds will tend to devote their intellect to justifying their own view over understanding another's point of view. An extreme example of this is blaming rape victims for the way they dress. This attitude is very common where men are acculturated to be "macho."

Often in more traditional societies, external cultural rules exert a powerful restriction on how emotions can be expressed. Rules such as "real men don't cry" and all that this statement implies, along with their female corollaries, are still prevalent in many places.

In trying to conform, young people are often taught to try to use their minds to control their emotions in order to get praise and avoid punishment. From a physical perspective this makes perfect sense. However, before long, this type of conditioning leads to a clouding of the emotions. You like what you think you should like, and not what you really like, then you don't know what you like at all. Even worse, you convince yourself that you hate what you really like, so other people won't think you like the thing you are not supposed to like.

This behavior is self-defeating. If one uses the intellect to control the emotions in order to conform to an external situation, the creative life is reversed. Using the intellect to emotionally investigate the physical in service to CREATING your inner energetic vision of the external situation is how we are meant to live. Your reasoning mind will tell you this is TRUE if you think about it.

Feel What You Feel

The cure to the negative cultural conditioning that has plagued humanity for ages is as simple as it is obvious. You have to let yourself REALLY feel what you feel. Failure to do so will cause you endless psychic stress as the natural flow between the intellectual and the emotional gets blocked. People who enjoy material success sometimes have a harder time feeling their true emotions because they have more toys to distract themselves. A rich man has a mid-life crisis, and will maybe get a red sports car. That will not help for very long... A poor man has a mid-life crisis, and maybe it will lead to some serious introspection and reflection that will change his entire outlook of life.

It is vitally important to understand how emotions help the intellect investigate the physical in order to bring forth inner qualities from beyond thinking. Let's say, a young man named Lance discovers that he likes to dance. Having supportive parents and trusting in his own feelings, he follows the attraction. The feeling gets stronger and it becomes his passion and he majors in Dance. Eventually, Lance entrances France with his prancing dance called "Running La Mans." Most importantly, Lance is living an inner-directed life.

Contrast Lance to his less fortunate neighbor, Matt who also liked dance. His dad said "you should go play football like I did." Lacking the knowledge to know better, and already laden with the ability to maintain a false emotional front for his "old man," Matt goes in for football. He is good at it. He gets a football scholarship and even goes pro. After a decent career, he retires comfortably. Matt identifies himself as a physical being and is emotionally stuck. He is not a happy person and hates his dad (but he pretends to love him).

Okay, these **hypotheticals** are exaggerated for fun and effect, and rarely is anyone so two dimensional. But here is the point, only Lance was able to live an inner directed life. Was it luck? Was it good parents? I know since they <u>live in my imagination</u> - it is because only Lance read my book!

To "feel what you feel" is not as easy to do as it is to say. To begin with, how many people are completely honest even to themselves about their feelings? Ever hear someone say, "I don't dare hope because the disappointment would kill me." Or how about, "I would vote for him, but he can't win." In both cases, the intellect is restricted by fear of a physical likelihood (I'll be disappointed; he won't win) and respond by redirecting their natural emotional reaction into something else.

People caught in situations like this, where the "mind" and the "heart" are in conflict most often start to self-anesthetize in one way or another as the disparity gets too large for them to handle. This can take the form of illegal drugs, legal prescriptions (often more powerful than the illegal ones when taken in high dosage), escapist behavior, mental alienation, or the most socially acceptable method, alcohol. By going for the Big Numb, the mind, the heart and the body are united, albeit in a death-like shadow of a conscious unity. At least, it is quiet.

PERSONAL INTERLUDE: Beijing, China, September of 1998.

It's the same party where I am later seated next Ms. X, but earlier in the evening before the guest of honor arrives. Growing up in California, I was not into Chinese music. Ironically, it was while I was in Tokyo that I discovered Mandarin Pop and at that time a certain singer who moved from Beijing to launch her career in Hong Kong was the reigning queen. I fell hard for her lilting melodies and she became my soundtrack for a few years. To my surprise, when I get to the party, I see her playing mahjong with some other (lesser) stars.

I play it cool and thanks to my unusual job (at least in their circles) at the American Embassy, I am a mini-attraction, and SHE comes over to talk to ME. After some casual conversation, I can tell that everyone there is already "three sheets to the wind." She asks why I'm not drinking. I prevaricate but finally confess it is because I am investigating a religion and trying to live by its tenants while I am doing so. One of them is no alcohol. She stares at me blankly. I quickly add that mainly it is for improving one's clarity of mind.

She takes a drag on her cigarette and rolls her eyes. With more honesty then perhaps she means to express, she says softly "Why? Clarity is so painful."

People fear feeling things that if they really faced them, they would have to change something in their life that they don't want to. The mistake in such thinking is that only by facing the feeling they fear will they EVER be able to change the things in their life that they DO want to.

Three years after we met, I read that my "idol" was getting a divorce from her then husband, a mainland musician. I met him once while they were married... He asked me to help his "female actress friend..." get a visa to do a screen test with Richard Gere. I told him I was in the Administrative Section of the Embassy not the Consular Section. It's kind of like asking the water department to take away the trash. They divorced soon after that.

My favorite singer went on to a "controversial" relationship (Hong Kong being quite a conventional society in many ways) with a younger man, a Hong Kong actor, singer and now producer. After a long and winding road, they are now reportedly going to be married.

Sorry for the digression, but this couple is actually a very good example of people who become more self-assured and centered (not self-centered) as they get older, and I am sure "feel what you feel" is something that they have learned to do.

And with centeredness and self-assurance comes the next logical thing to do...

Reclaim Your Power

Why do we do anything? Most people separate things they do into two piles: things they have to do, and things they want to do. You suffer the work you don't like, to get the vacation you do like. This is an illusion. There is only one pile, doing whatever you are going to do, once you make up your mind to do it. If you are doing what you truly want to do, that intention will infuse every part of your doing with meaning.

If it is YOUR first place to live by yourself then even cleaning the toilet takes on a new significance.

Putting the "thing" you want first (the physical goal) makes everything leading up to it seem like a chore. Remember the ice skating champion who hired someone to break her competitor's leg? Could it be that deep down, she didn't even really like skating, only being champion?

Why do we do something we don't want to? Mostly fear of a negative consequence.

And here we arrive at the crux of the question. Life is usually pretty obvious. You DO have to do a lot of things just to survive, but the important moments in life are when things almost balance out and you have to make a meaningful choice. Things are going well enough, so why try something new and risk losing face or (worst of all) losing "everything?" There is only one answer - because the authentic YOU demand it. This is not the outward-directed ego "little you." Breaking convention in one's family, culture, profession, or whatever, is never easy, and failure could be as bad as you fear.

However, outward success and failure are only happenings in the physical level. On the emotional level, it is about being true to your feelings. Being made the king of the world, only to cry inside "I didn't want this," is a very sad plight. Or as a wise football coach once said, "It is not about winning or losing. It's about how you play the game."

I knew the nephew of the then seventh richest man in Hong Kong. His uncle wanted to groom him to take over the company as his uncle never had children. My friend didn't go for it. He wanted to be his own man. Last time I saw him he was working his ass off, but had time for three girlfriends.

People sometimes do what is "expected" of them, thinking that doing so will make them happy. This is rarely true and when it is, usually it is because what was expected of them happened to coincide with what they themselves internally wanted to do anyway.

There once were three Chinese-American brothers. Their parents wanted one to be a doctor, one to be an engineer, and one to be a lawyer. The first son dutifully got a junior helper job at the local hospital to learn the ropes. The first day he sees an old man go into cardiac arrest and the doctors had to perform open heart massage to save the patient. He knew he didn't want to be a doctor right there because he realized he really didn't like the sight of blood. He is doing great today in another profession.

The second brother obediently got into the sciences and the first time he saw a computer, he was hooked. He got into a good engineering program and never looked back. He rode the tech revolution tide and became a highly paid electronics engineer in the Silicon Valley. Today through considering the logical conclusions necessitated by quantum physics, he is starting to meditate more and "computate" less (I am revising the meaning of this archaic word, made obsolete by "compute", to mean humans who think compulsively in a pre-programmed way).

The third brother didn't really care for law school, but agreed to go that way to please his parents, and he thought law school could be plan B. But secretly he had another plan all along and lucky for him, the plan worked out very well. The moral of the story is that all three brothers went on to live happily ever after because they all knew the wisdom of "follow your heart."

Or as Obi Wan said to Luke Skywalker, "trust your feelings."

To learn from an extreme example, let us consider the plight of the true martyr. I am NOT talking about suicide bombers. The true martyr is not being asked to kill themselves, but only to do something that he or she would rather die than do.

True martyrdom can understandably have a powerful effect in material reality through the clear demonstration that the martyr values something non-physical more than their mortal life. Through the perception and meaning given to their action by others, martyrs often spark revolutions in social and political environments overburdened with injustice. However, as the saying goes, "Please, don't be a martyr." You can't fake something that extreme. On the other hand, if being one is coming from your deepest level of being, well, you know what I would say then…

Let me take time to say a few words about post-traumatic stress disorder (PTSD) and other related mental issues here. I have had the privilege to meet and assist in the recovery of a few people suffering from this malady. The common thread seems to me to be the inability of the mind to control the recurrence (or even moderate the intensity) of painful memories. The memories have such vivid emotional intensity that it overwhelms the physical senses, and take the person back in time to the moment of the trauma, forcing them to relive it over and over. Unfortunately, I did not have the opportunity to continue treating these people for any extended period of time. My limited experience in this area reinforced my initial impression that the "cure" would not come from applying medication (especially anti-psychotics with their unknown side effects), nor would it likely come from conventional talk psychotherapy.

The heart knows what it wants

PERSONA INTERLUDE – Beijing, China, November of 2001.

I am sitting on a plane at Beijing International Airport. So glad to be going back south where it is at least a bit warmer. I made the mistake of letting my friend talk me into flying up for the weekend to have "Peking duck" at a new restaurant. He does this kind of thing all the time as he is one of those wealthy, jet-set type guys. I would usually never do something so frivolous, but something hit me and I said "why not try something new." Well, big mistake (or so it seemed)!

The restaurant was overbooked, and we had to wait a long time. The duck was not all that great, and they didn't even have roasted scorpions appetizers, so hardly what I would call authentic. Also I didn't bring enough clothes and it was so cold. Then we get bumped and then had to hang out at the airport for hours. Finally, we pay extra to get some seats in first class just to get home Sunday night so I can be at work the next day. Sitting in first class, I hear the announcement that we will be delayed on the runway so please remain seated.

I am tired, and bored so I start looking around. Looking back through the space between the seats, I see a young woman in business class. Suddenly, it's like I hear my own voice saying in my head: "I know her. She looks so familiar. Sure, she is beautiful, but that's not it." I was sure I have never met her (in this lifetime). Then I think, I MUST MEET HER.

So I come up with this elaborate scheme to introduce myself without seeming like a total lothario. We date for a few months then we break up partly due to the fact we lived on two different continents. A few years later we run into each other again. Nine years after our initial meeting, we get married.

Throughout literary history, star-crossed lovers are a favorite theme. How the hopeless pair's inevitable fall into the non-physical (death) enthrall the readers' sympathies! Romeo and Juliet in the west, the "Butterfly Lovers" in the east, the story is the same, the heart knows what it wants, and no material obstacle or reasoned argument is going to change it.

The heart's power to overcome physical and mental obstacles in tragic love stories like Romeo and Juliet is what attracts us to them. However, these situations don't really happen all that much, and when they they do, they often don't come to such dramatic conclusions as people tend to be more practical in the real world. Such stories derive their mythical power precisely from the fact that they don't happen in everyday life, but infuse our lives with a deeper meaning and a yearning to believe they CAN happen.

The intersection of parental authority and misguided emotional control over their children is the engine that drives both the fictional tragedies of great literature as well as real life cases of star-crossed lovers. Often the parents will couch their opposition in terms of love for the child, and not wanting them to suffer over an "impossible" situation. Like the parents in the famous movie, "Guess Who Is Coming To Dinner?" they think they know what is best for their children. Unfortunately, what they fail to understanding is that what they are doing is projecting their fears into a future that they themselves are helping to perpetuate.

PERSONAL INTERLUDE: San Francisco, July of 1998.

I am home in California on vacation and get a chance to tell my mom about declaring as a member of the Baha'i Faith. I go on and on about all the reasons. She just listens. After I realize she is not REALLY listening. I stop. "Do you have any questions?"

"Is it a cult?"

"No." I try another approach. "One of the teachings is that single Baha'is must have the approval of their parents in order to get married, but their parents can't choose whom they marry. It's like...a veto."

"This is a good religion!"

When parental control runs amok, as this item, ripped from the headlines shows, the heart turned in on itself can fester and lead to such horrific outcomes that we all want to look away and just say, "we can never understand why." But we can understand, and we must understand. Why is it that loving the wrong person is still so deadly? Ultimately, the reasons come from... within.

The case involves the tradition of "honor killing" in Pakistan. The outside world first learned of the details on January 16, 2017 when the high court in Lahore sentenced a woman to death for burning her daughter alive in June of 2016 for marrying a man of her choice in eastern Pakistan.

I will piece together the story for you from various press reports. Parveen Bibi was convicted of burning to death her own daughter, Zeenat Rafiq, a week after her marriage to Hassan Khan. The court sentenced Anees Rafique to life in prison for helping his mother kill his 18-year-old sister.

Authorities say Bibi brought Rafiq back home with a promise of celebrating the wedding but burned her alive instead.

Neighbors in the congested, working-class neighborhood in the sprawling eastern Pakistani city came running when they heard the screams, but family members kept them from entering the house. When police eventually arrived and found the charred body near a staircase they arrested the mother.

The victim's husband told reporters the two had been "in love since our school days" but the family had rejected several marriage proposals, forcing them to elope. Khan told Pakistani media that his wife had only returned to her own family for a visit after being assured it would be a celebration of her marriage, and she would not be harmed. He said he agreed reluctantly to let her return.

A local police official said Parveen confessed to killing her daughter with the help of her son Ahmar. He quoted the woman as saying "I don't have any regrets." Another police officer said the body showed signs of beating and strangulation.

For generations now in Pakistan, they've called it "honor" killing, carried out in the name of a family's reputation. The killers routinely invoke Islam, but can never cite anything other than their belief that

Islam doesn't allow the mixing of sexes. Even Pakistan's hard-line Islamic Ideology Council which is hardly known for speaking out to protect women says the practice defies Islamic tenets. In the vast majority of cases, the "honor" killer is a man and the victim is a woman.

The victim is often a sister who falls in love with a man not of her family's choosing and dares to follow her heart; a daughter who refuses to agree to an arranged marriage (sometimes to a much older man she has never met); a wife who can no longer stay in an abusive marriage and divorces her husband legally.

The killer is often someone who cannot bear the taunts of other men brought up as he was, believing that women are subservient and must be kept in the shadows, their worth often measured by the number of sons they can produce. He thinks all of his neighbors also think there is nothing wrong in taking the life of a woman who "steps out of line." He is someone who is not sad at having to kill his own family member because she is already "dead to him." He is someone who is glad that death will "wash" the "dishonor" from other members of the family.

If it is considered an honor to kill in such a way and have it be considered normal human behavior, who is at fault? Why does it continue? Who confers the honor once it is done? Is it the neighbors? Is it the rest of the family? Is it society?

This particularly case illustrates that we are all responsible for our choices. Choice brings consequence. Even when we say we are compelled by social and cultural forces, the decision to act is an internal one. As I meditate on this particular "honor killing," I began to get an impression that the real motive here was jealousy. A mother jealous of her own child's freedom and happiness, something she perhaps never tasted or even allowed herself to dream of. How many other such killings are motivated by similar feelings hiding behind an excuse of social compulsion?

The child in this case had made her choice and left. Whatever dishonor there was has passed. To lure her back with a false promise only to kill her with the (willing?) assistance of her own brother is the kind of meticulous planning that comes with cold calculation. To claim any kind of religious sanction is ridiculous as the press reports show, even the MOST conservative religious leaders in the country condemn these horror killings.

The mom is responsible for her choice. The daughter is responsible for her choice of trusting and returning, hoping against hope to unite her family. The physical consequence for the mother was a death sentence. The physical consequence for the daughter was also a death sentence. The emotional consequence for the mother is too dreadful for me to contemplate. The emotional consequence for the daughter could well be seen as a victory of conviction. As the pain passed and her physicality ended, she achieved the victory of following her heart.

Yes, the killing happened because she loved the wrong person - by which I mean the mother loved herself way too much.

There was NO religious reason to do this. There was apparently little or no social pressure as they lived in a poor, but urban area where the custom is dying out. The father was not mentioned as an instigator so the usual "male" dominance factor seems to be not at work here. So what motivated the mother was coming from… within.

"No," you say, "such a thing can't be caused by jealousy!" Social pressure, backwardness, culture must be responsible. This is Pakistan, for god's sake. It can't happen in America!

Let us review the details of another tragedy that took place in New York in 2013 before you jump to any conclusions. When I was asked by *Sing Tao* Radio, the Chinese language network, to talk about the possible psychological motivations behind these killings, I did a detailed review of the available media coverage and intensely reflected on the issues at hand.

From English and Chinese press reports, this is what apparently happened in October of 2013. Just before the tragedy unfolded, phone calls in rapid succession, each call more frantic than the last, were made by a woman surnamed Li, warning her relatives that her husband's 25-year-old cousin, who had been staying with their family, was acting strange.

By the time other family members came to her home in Sunset Park to investigate, it was too late. Inside the apartment, the woman, Qiao Zhen Li, lay unconscious in the kitchen, next to her 5-year-old son, both were mortally wounded. The bodies of her three other children, all hacked to death, were in a rear bedroom.

The relatives had to break the door down and when they finally got inside on that Saturday night, they came upon the carnage, and the man responsible, Chen Mingdong, covered in blood. They took the murder weapon from an unresisting Chen and called the police. Mr. Chen was arrested and charged with five counts of murder.

The killings cut through the close knit extended family like a scythe through wheat and five people were gone. The small three-room home on 57th Street, where the children and their parents lived a poor, but seemingly happy life stood out for only the lack of anything special. Their very happiness was what appeared to have grated on Chen Mingdong, who lived an impoverished and itinerant life between Chinatowns in Manhattan and Chicago before moving in with his cousin in Sunset Park.

The woman who was killed had warned relatives about Chen's troubling behavior. Under interrogation by detectives, conducted in Mandarin, he told of his disillusionment with life since coming to the United States in 2004 and of his jealousy toward those who had found success here. But it remained unclear to the public and even to the family that he was a part of, what prompted him to turn his rage on his cousin's wife and her four children.

The police said Chen appeared to have stayed with them before without incident. The family did not appear to be better-off than those who lived around them in their Chinese enclave near Ninth Avenue in Brooklyn. They sent their three school-age children to a local public school, and Ms. Li stayed at home with the youngest child. The authorities had no record of troubles in the household. A cousin of the mother told reporters after the murders that Mr. Chen was emotionally unstable but did not elaborate.

The only weapon used in the killings, the police said, was a large kitchen knife, described by the authorities as a meat cleaver. The police reported that the bodies "were cut and butchered" and that most of the wounds were to the neck and torso. The nature of the attack, using a kitchen implement, pointed to spontaneity, and the number killed surprised even veteran investigators.

It was not clear what may have precipitated the killings in the Sunset Park apartment or what caused Ms. Li to become alarmed. Chen had no prior arrests in New York, and did not appear to have had trouble with the law in Chicago. Investigators believed that Chen, who does not speak English, had not left the United States since arriving here many years ago. During the interrogation, Mr. Chen spoke in general of feelings of resentment.

The police revealed that Chen made a comment that since he's been in this country, "everyone seems to be doing better than him."

There was no trial as Chen pled guilty to three counts of second-degree murder and two counts of first-degree manslaughter. He was originally charged with five counts of first-degree murder.

"I only would have accepted this plea if never again under any circumstances could he be free in society," said the judge as he sentenced Chen to 125 years in prison.

The only glimpse of a motive for the killings that Chen ever offered remains the single comment that "everyone seems to be doing better than him" since his arrival in the United States.

Mark Hale, an assistant district attorney, explained why prosecutors had agreed to the plea this way, "the burning question is why these things happen, but in the sum total of things it doesn't matter. It is a certainty that the goal of public safety will be accomplished. This man will be permanently removed from society, and it saves the family an ordeal of a trial."

When the dead woman's sister-in-law asked Hale through the interpreter, "Did he tell you why he did it?" The prosecutor could only shake his head.

Public presupposition was this was a poor, uneducated immigrant, who didn't fit in. He snapped for "no reason."

According to the more detailed coverage in the Chinese press, family members were crying and yelling out at the sentencing in Chinese, "Just tell us why! Tell us why!" Chen just sat "stone faced."

In fact, Chen had confessed the reason why when he "softly" told them, according to the words of the investigators, that it was because, "since he arrived *everyone* seems to be doing better than him." His cousin, not so different in a physical sense in terms of age, background, even looks, has *everything* - wife, kids, job. "Everyone" is no one. His cousin is someone he can identify with.

Chen wanted Chinatown to fit the American dream he harbored in his long wait to join his family. But what he found was a world where he could not even get a busboy job in Chinatown because Mexican boys work for less and can speak enough "Putonghua" (standard Chinese) to get the job done. Chen's Fujian accent marked him as a bumpkin (in his mind).

As he appeared to be totally materially oriented, Chen could find no outlet for the negative feelings brought on by his material failure. Instead of reading to expand his mind, listening to music, exploring America, or playing with the kids, being a good "uncle," he began to isolate himself. Seeing what he does not have is painful deep in his heart. Over time, the pain starts to become untenable.

He starts to deaden all of his emotions as he a way to deal with what is happening inside and it is probably around this time that the family members begin to notice him keeping to himself, not talking, avoiding eye contact.

The more he tries to NOT feel the feelings, the more MENTAL attention he has to pay to not feeling them. The more mental attention he pays to not feeling them, the more powerful they become. Finally, his "ingrown heart" can bear it no more.

He can only destroy the things that cause him pain. He will make it so that his cousin will also not have the things he can't have…

Certainly these are pure suppositions on my part, but it sure beats the DA's summary, "The burning question is why these things happen, but in the sum total of things it doesn't matter."

And if anyone still thinks the underlying cause for the killings is poverty or lack of a job (not enough material things), let me remind you of Joseph Lyle Menéndez (born 1968) and Erik Galen Menéndez (born 1970). The brothers are known for their conviction in 1994, as a result of a much-publicized trial, for the murders of their wealthy parents, entertainment executive Jose Menéndez and his wife Mary "Kitty" Menéndez of Beverly Hills, California, in 1989.

They were sentenced to life imprisonment without the possibility of parole. Jose was shot point-blank in the back of the head with a 12-gauge shotgun. Kitty, awakened by the shots, sprang from the couch and ran for the hallway but was shot in the leg. She slipped in her own blood and fell, and then was shot several times in the arm, chest, and face, leaving her unrecognizable. Both Jose and Kitty were then shot in the kneecap in an attempt to make the murders appear related to organized crime.

The apparent motive was the brothers wanted their inheritance sooner rather than later. The actual cause in my opinion is "materialism poisoning." Whatever was really in the minds of these killers - jealousy, greed, or just cold blooded disregard for one's own family, it came from... within.

Understanding WHY these crimes happen is EXACTLY what matters here. These are crimes that are caused by emotional sickness. Emotional sickness is NOT caused by emotional germs. It is not caused by society, though some societies do offer a good breeding ground for the cause.

The cause is not something that happens suddenly. The cause is the result of a very long list of bad decisions, and reinforcing these decisions, even as experience tells us differently, that material things will solve emotional problems. Understanding that this is NOT so, is the only way to overcome emotional illness.

When someone is in emotion pain, to try to feel better through a physical approach is self-defeating. For someone who only knows material ways to be happy, they imagine if they had this or that thing, THEN "I will be happy." If they don't get it, they don't want anyone else to get it either!

My father-in-law said something wise to me, but he did not come up with it. "When you are in a deep hole, first stop digging."

The heart knows what it wants, but when that wanting is turned into a material dead end, it will fester and become sick.

When you feel depressed, the first thing is to stop being depressed that you are depressed. When you feel jealous over someone's happiness, the first thing is to stop thinking about YOURSELF. Be happy that happiness exists and you are able to even imagine what it is. People who say they want to be happy "more than anything," and thinks getting someone to do something or obtaining something will make them happy has no idea what happiness is. It is a myth to them. They don't know what being happy would be like, and if they actually felt it, on some level, it would be recognized as "this is new!"

People who fail to see that happiness is not a destination, but just another emotion that signals something will have a hard time recognizing it when it does come into their lives. Happiness comes from aligning your mental direction with your emotional flow and striving to make it become a material reality. It is NOT the material outcome that causes the happiness one feels when it becomes real. Happiness can still come when you truly follow your heart's desire and the outcome is not what you wanted as long as you are not dead set on one particular outcome, but recognize that it is the striving to be true to yourself that brings happiness.

Chen Mingdong's 125 years and the Menendez brothers' life sentences are their physical punishment. The emotional and psychological punishment is for them to work out. However, the physical is always moving on, and unless the deeper lessons are taken in, all they can see with their eyes is all they have got inside. Then before long, they will move on, no wiser.

I am reminded of the Baha'i teaching: *"O SON OF SPIRIT! Noble have I created thee, yet thou hast abased thyself. Rise then unto that for which thou wast created."*

I have a theory that being so close to the physical level, emotions can have a powerful effect on the laws of physical reality. Emotions might well be able to "bend" the rules of physical reality more than we realize...

It has even been suggested that when strong emotions arise due to violence or regret at the time of death this can "make" someone become a ghost. Disturbingly, there are black magic belief systems which suggest that killing people in certain ways can allow the black magician to make them into "slave ghosts." Based on personal experience, I believe the ghost phenomenon must be related to emotional energy in some way.

The history of the ghost phenomenon shows that ghosts seem to exist "outside" of time (they persist through long period of time and do not observe the second law of thermodynamics), but interestingly they appear to remain tied to space, a specific place or more rarely an object or a person. I will not speculate further on the nature of ghosts, and simply say that while some appear to be linked to a deceased individual human with a discernable life story others appear to be less human, lacking even a human form. All that there is sometimes is emotion - an overriding emotion. A sense of hunger or a desire that can never be satisfied…

PERSONAL INTERLUDE: Shenzhen SEZ (Special Economic Zone), China, February of 1996.

After Japan, I was assigned to the Consulate in Guangzhou. In Japan, and even in Taiwan, I stood out as the "Chinese-American." It was great to be able to blend in like a native and hear what people REALLY think since my Cantonese is still native enough that I can pass as one.

I've just started seeing someone new, and we are going to Hong Kong for a short trip, but this is 1996 and the border closes much earlier than now. We are running late as we left on a Friday night after work and I am already tired from the work week and the hour too long drive to the border didn't help…

"My head grows heavy and my sight grows dim, I have to stop for the night."

So I randomly pick a nearby hotel for us and am glad they didn't overcharge for not having a reservation. We get to the room…

"…as she stood in the doorway, I hear the mission bell. And I'm thinking to myself…"

God, this place smells like hell!

The stench of tobacco odor is overwhelming. We are both pretty hungry, I figure we will just open the window and come back later.

Well, a couple hours after we had the window open, go out for a bite and come back, the smell is still very strong. I call the front desk to see if they have another room. They are sorry, but this is it. Since it is almost midnight, I say screw it and we call it a night.

Sometime shortly after we both fall asleep, I think I feel a draft (we kept the window cracked open as the smell is so strong) and wake up.

Or did I? Everything looks the same… I am lying in bed… she's sleeping on my left arm… Why is it so dark? It's like even the street lights have gone out…

Wait, why is that corner over there getting… darker?

The blackness of the dark room gets even more so in that corner. Then a portion of it starts to stretch outward, slowly at first, like cold honey being poured out, then suddenly faster. The darkness stretches out like an arm and quickly takes on a tent-like form of absolute darkness about 5 feet tall.

I see it from the bed as I raise myself halfway up, my arm still pinned down by the sleeping woman next to me. I feel… bemused. I watch the form approach. It seems "surprised" to notice I am sitting up in bed.

I take a closer look and the best I can say is that it looks like a small man cloaked in a black sheet. There is no face to speak of and there isn't even the shape of shoulders or arms under the "black sheet." On closer inspection, I can see the "sheet" is so dark it seems to suck in the little bit of light that is shining on it and make the room darker, but it has a strange luster, like oil on water.

The "he" speaks! I say he because as I half lie there with one arm pinned, I hear a man's voice with my ears, and it seems to come from the "thing." In Cantonese, he says, "I want to possess your body and have sex with that woman."

At this point, you would think I would realize "OH, it's a dream!" or be scared awake.

Instead, I say in a very steady if a bit haughty tone, "Do you know who my dad is?"

"Do you want me to call him down here and kick your ass?" I continue, also in Cantonese.

The thing acts like it doesn't hear me and creeps closer…

"Fine, you are going to make me take out my left hand and do it myself!" I start to move my arm from under my companion…

The thing starts to retreat, slowly at first then… all at once it shrinks back into the corner. The room looks more normal and the street lights are now visible.

I lie back down and close my eyes. It seems like only a minute later and it is morning. My left arm is numb.

Later I mention to some friends in Shenzhen where I had stayed and they were surprised I had not heard about the place's history. It seems I had checked into a famous haunted hotel that was built over what used to be the execution grounds during the Japanese occupation. I wondered if what I saw had anything to do with that, but strangely, I never gave it much thought. I never even mentioned it to my companion that evening, and only much later, I shared it as a funny story with family.

The woman who slept on my arm acted like nothing happened and mentioned nothing, so I guess nothing happened to her.

To summarize what we have discussed in these first two steps, let me share with you my suggestions for avoiding a materially driven life:

On the physical level, you must be willing to try new things. Do NOT fixate on a material goal! You might or might not like the new things, but you will learn something, and you will never know what they could lead to.

On the emotional level, you have to learn to really let yourself feel what you feel. Then let it go. Use the emotional truth as it comes to you to make up your mind about what to do.

Then JUST GO FOR IT (Nike might have copyrighted the other saying).

However, "just go for it" is a not a simple mental exercise. Before you can "just go for it," a lot of things have to happen in the mind. Decisions don't just grow on some kind of thought tree, you know.

Chapter Four

THE THIRD STEP

You are not your thoughts

Before we dive into the realm of thoughts, consider this last thing about the realm of emotions. Is it not true that no matter how out of control you have felt, however much you gave in to some emotion, your awareness was there? If it wasn't, you have a legal defense for what you did! Otherwise, you made a decision to empower your emotion, and not your awareness. I use the word awareness here only in the sense of thoughtful deliberation, conscious mindfulness of the events happening, a form of intellectual awareness.

If emotions only derive meaning from how we think about the cause of the feelings, what gives rise to the thoughts? How is it that we are aware of the world in the first place?

Let us now consider the intellectual realm that seems to be uniquely human and distinct from all of the other creatures on this planet. If we share the emotional world with animals, how is it that we "see" the world in a way that solves the problem of converting light into ideas? We have eyes that evolved along the same path as animals and ours are in no way as acute as many of them, so it must be something "behind" the eyes.

How is it that human beings can overcome the problem of visually understanding features and objects in the world that are so complex that it is a task far beyond the abilities of the world's most powerful computers (for now). Let's take a moment to review what we know about human vision. Human vision requires distilling foreground from background, recognizing objects presented in a wide range of orientations, and accurately interpreting spatial cues. The neural mechanisms of visual perception offer rich insight into how the human brain handles such computationally complex situations.

Visual perception begins as soon as the eye focuses light onto the retina, where it is absorbed by a layer of photoreceptor cells. These receptor cells convert light into electrochemical signals, and are divided into two types, rods and cones, named for their shape.

Cone cells are responsible for color vision and function best in relatively bright light, as opposed to rod cells, which work better in low light. Cone cells are densely packed in the fovea centralis, a 0.3 mm diameter rod-free area with very thin, densely packed cones which quickly reduce in number towards the periphery of the retina. Rod cells are responsible for our night vision, and are found mostly in the peripheral regions of the retina, so most people will find that they can see better at night if they focus their gaze just off to the side of whatever they are looking at.

Most projections from the retina travel via the optic nerve to a part of the thalamus called the lateral geniculate nucleus (LGN), deep in the center of the brain. The LGN separates retinal inputs into parallel streams, one containing color and fine structure, and the other containing contrast and motion. Cells that process color and fine structure make up the top four of the six layers of the LGN. These cells project all the way to the back of the brain to primary visual cortex (V1).

Every newborn baby has a hypertrophy, or overgrowth, of haphazard connections in the brain which must be carefully pruned, based on visual experience, into crisply defined columns. It is actually a reduction in the number of connections (not an increase) that improves the infant's ability to see fine detail and to recognize shapes and patterns. This type of activity dependent refinement is not limited to V1, but occurs in many areas throughout the cerebral cortex.

At the same time that the ability to discriminate lines and edges is improving in primary visual cortex, cells in secondary visual cortex (V2), are refining their ability to interpret colors. V2 is largely responsible for the phenomenon of color constancy, which explains the fact that a red rose still looks red to us under many different colors of illumination. Color constancy is thought to occur because V2 can compare an object and the ambient illumination, and can subtract out the estimated illumination color. This process is strongly influenced by what color the viewer expects the object to be. In fact, almost all higher order features of vision are influenced by expectations based on past experience.

This characteristic extends to color and form perception in V3 and V4, to face and object recognition in the inferior temporal lobe, and to motion and spatial awareness in the parietal lobe. Although such influences occasionally allow the brain to be fooled into misperception, as is the case with optical illusions, they also give us with the ability to see and respond to the visual world very quickly.

From the detection of light and dark in the retina, to the abstraction of lines and edges in V1, to the interpretation of objects and their spatial relationships in higher visual areas, each task in visual perception illustrates the efficiency and strength of the human visual system.

Did you know all that happens when light enters our eyes?

So, the physical brain is pared down in infancy by our reaction to (primarily through physical vision, then emotional input, and later psychological interpretation) outside stimulus. Later in life, what we think we see is strongly influenced by what we EXPECT to see. Ultimately, everything in our physical experience is like that.

Our perception of everything external is based on a psychological interpretation of a physical nerve impulse delivered to the brain that then becomes your inner impression. Theoretically, you could be lying in a coma and with enough bandwidth and a good enough connection to your brain, you could be made to see or feel just about anything.

In other words, our perception is completely colored by what we expect to perceive. How then can we know our perceptions are not deceptions? Or as Morpheus said to Neo in the movie The Matrix, "You think that's air you're breathing?" Or as Tom Campbell might say, "You know that's only a virtual brain you are sensing electrical signals with."

Whatever we see, we see... within. As amazingly fast as the body is in delivering light signals into nerve energy that can be converted into ideas, it is amazingly slow compared to the speed of thoughts themselves. The speed of light is roughly 299,792,458 meters per second. What is the speed of thought?

Someone who is stuck on over identification with their bodies and those who are emotionally stuck, manifest being "stuck" in their minds. Everything that happens to us happens within the "matrix" of our own minds.

Everything we experience, we experience **WITHIN**.

If you are limited to believing the waking experience of the outer world is all that there is, then you are limited to a world of your own making, crafted to fool you into thinking you are a physical body driven by emotional needs only to survive and procreate. You can grow up from that of course, but not everyone is ready for that.

In my experience, almost everyone confuses what they think with what they see in some area of life. Unless they can "see" deeper, what they can see will be limited to what they think they see. To feel a form of "awakening" for someone like this is relatively easy. They simply have to notice what was there the whole time, but beyond their external vision, for the first time!

A very material man awakens to the suffering of others, and has an emotional breakthrough. A very emotional man learns to understand the source of his trauma, and has an intellectual awakening. A very thoughtful man awakens to his deeper energetic nature and looks… within.

Looking within by a physically, emotionally and intellectually prepared person leads naturally to another kind of "awakening." This kind of awakening is where you awaken to a new WAY to perceive. Then you can begin to perceive information that is beyond physical seeing, emotional feeling, and even mental imagining.

However, most people today, are stuck in "thinking" and are addicted (in the medical sense) to thinking. **They are "trapped" in the matrix of their own mind.** They mentally dissect everything that happens to them to reach some judgment about what that means to THEM. In others words, they are constantly in a reaction mode, and they ONLY see what they EXPECT to see.

This kind of mind endlessly generates speculation based on external data. It starts to create its own mental model of everything it can't directly touch to "get a handle" on the situation (like what other people are REALLY thinking). At the extreme end of the spectrum, sometimes called "excessive ideation", non-stop thought creation can literally "drive you crazy."

Envision a Congress that endlessly debates itself and is detached from reality and ignorant of the world of regular people. It perceives only what it already believes and what decisions that do make it out of this "Capitol Hill" are dripping with hypocrisy, and corrupted by self-interest. This is an analogy of such a mind.

Let me try another of my five part metaphors for the essential human being here. Your body is the exterior of the car (the body), your emotions are the tires (where the rubber meets the road), your mind is all the mechanisms of the car (most importantly, the engine), your energy is of course the fuel, and the being-level you is the driver.

Excessive ideation would be analogous to a runaway engine, detached from the drive and burning itself out.

Some people just want a nice looking car that looks great sitting in the driveway; no engine, and it never goes anywhere. Some people want a great ride; smooth, good road contact, and road safety. Some people are all about tricking everything out; they can't work on the engine enough. In all cases, not much happens without gas in the tank. Unfortunately, like the animation movie "Cars," there are no drivers in sight. Drivers might exist, but they are mostly only read about in books on metaphysics.

People addicted to thinking endlessly try to mentally give "meaning" to all the events happening around them by trying to figure out how the events make them feel. The don't reflect on why they feel these feelings and simply push the reason for why they feel these feelings back into the world of things, and are constantly thinking about how they can influence events to get what they want. They mistake their thought projection for reality and permanently live in mental reaction to outside events that dictate how they feel.

Does this describe someone you know?

More than the sum of the parts

In the time since you have read about and incorporated the ideas related to steps one and two, I hope you have found a chance to really think about how these ideas apply to your life, and have started doing what you are inspired to do to experiment with them. It is very helpful for you to have already taken steps towards getting some "body knowing" and try to "feel what you feel" before we plunge ahead. If you find that you are stuck on difficult relationships (like I was), let me share something that I learned during a deep meditative state.

PERSONAL INTERLUDE – Some Place... Some Time...

The instructor points to a circle that appears as light suspended in the air. Your experience is like this circle, he says. I nod my head. Split it in half and turn one half over, like this. The circle of light does that as he speaks. Reconnect the ends so they look like this. He points; the circle is now a sine wave pattern. I intuit that we need to stop seeing just our own point of view, and try (there is no try, there is only do or do not) to also see the other person's point of view. Then depending of the depth of our seeing, that is how big the change will be. Some very elaborate formula about how the trajectories of the emotions can be calculated based on the length of the wave... Unconscious...

Let me put it another way... Picture this...

Saint Peter goes on a break at the Pearly Gates, he asks baby Jesus to take over for a minute. A "bad" banker mistakenly shows up and he has no chance of getting in even though he convinced himself people willingly invested their money (... and it's gone).

Baby Jesus, "Hey mister, I don't see a medal on you, which kind of entry pass do you have, silver or gold?" (SILVER: Do Not Hurt Others in Ways that Would Hurt You. GOLD: Do Unto Others As You Would Have Them Do Unto You.)

Banker, "Well, kid, I made a ton of money. I can buy whatever I need to get in."

Baby Jesus, "You CAN'T buy it. You need to "be" gold or silver or you don't get in.

Banker, "There has to be exceptions? A backdoor…"

Baby Jesus, "Well, we do make exceptions for people who hurt others in their sincere belief they are protecting those who can't protect themselves, but you don't look like one of them…"

Banker, "Great, what kind of thing is that?"

Baby Jesus, "They have a copper medal, of course!

The "hand" wants to protect what it loves even if it has to be a FIST. The "head" knows that to protect what it loves, it has to not cause harm or give others cause to harm it. The "heart" only knows what it loves and what it loves is LOVE. And that is why the "heart" is the first class citizen in heaven.

Or as Maria from Fritz Lang's classic movie Metropolis (1927) puts it, "There can be no understanding between the hand and the brain unless the heart acts as mediator." The deep mystery of why the heart rules in heaven and not the head is that it is the core of the lower unity that leads to what comes later.

Because the rational mind is not JUST a combination of these three factors - hand, heart and head - it would be a misreading to say the mind is COMPOSED of these three aspects. Rather it is at the point we begin to harmonize and fully connect these three aspects that we begin to experience our least substantial aspect (of course it was always there).

Once the physical, emotional and intellectual basis exists, the higher rational mind appears, but we cannot say how this happens with any certainty. It is something that is more than the sum total of the parts. In a purely physical system, that would NOT be possible. What I am saying is this - physical reality (including the triune design of the human mind) did NOT evolve by random chance through particles hitting other particles to build it up over time via the process we call evolution. It evolved based on a set of rules established before there ever was any mass or energy (perhaps even space and time).

Emotions have a kind of body sensation, have "weight", and can be felt in an extremely physical way. Thoughts have less materiality, but we still speak of structures of thought and steps of logic. However, it is clear we have to acknowledge these are simply attempts to put a physical nomenclature onto a non-physical process.

Reflect inwardly on your thought process. Do you really create a new idea or are you just dissecting, processing, and discarding inputs that are coming to you from outside? Consider these quotes...

"I have nothing new to teach the world. Truth and Non-violence are as old as the hills. All I have done is to try experiments in both on as vast a scale as I could." --Mahatma Gandhi

"There is nothing new in the world except the history you do not know." -- Harry S Truman

"What has been is what will be, and what has been done is what will be done, and there is nothing new under the sun." -- Ecclesiastes 1:9

"We are second-hand people. We have lived on what we have been told, either guided by our inclinations, our tendencies, or compelled to accept by circumstances and environment. We are the result of all kinds of influences, and there is nothing new in us, nothing that we have discovered for ourselves: nothing original, pristine, clear." -- Jiddu Krishnamurti

Most of us base our value judgments on inclinations and prejudices acquired in childhood and we rarely revisit them. The mind is like a sponge that takes in everything that it experiences. If we limit ourselves to this level of the mind, it is hard to grow beyond the environment we find ourselves in.

However, we are not doomed to just repeat the past and be "second-hand people," and that is exactly what this book is about! If you stay on auto-pilot and play it safe, then you most likely will do just that. But as we proceed, you will learn there is a way out as this last quote intimates...

"Some people say there's nothing new under the sun. I still think that there's room to create, you know. And intuition doesn't necessarily come from under this sun. It comes from within." -- Pharrell Williams

Directed outward the intellect is like a knife that cuts up everything that it touches, so as to allow it to be better taken in. A delicate mind can be like a surgeon, and reason is the scalpel, but it can also be like a butcher and the intellect the cleaver. People who use their intellect to dominate others degrade themselves as well as their victims. When I see someone like that, I want to shout, "Watch out he has a psychic knife!"

A sharp mind lacking emotional sensitivity can hurt a lot of people without intending to and it can hurt many more people if the intention is to do so. Understanding that your mind is working best when it is working synergistically with your physical and emotional aspects is the greatest safeguard against the intellect becoming tyrannical.

Your intellect as a democracy

If your mind has three provinces called gut, heart and head, do they come together in a physical area of the body? No, of course not, they meet in the Capitol Dome of the great Parliament of the Mind, in the special district of DC (Direct Consciousness). This is where the rational mind we (at least some of us) are familiar with arises. This special place is where we determine who we are, what is real, and why and how we do what we do.

When Descartes declared that "I think therefore I am," he was speaking from the lobby of the Parliament.

Why does the personality sometimes seem like words carved in stone? Changing it seems well-nigh impossible! There is a Chinese saying to the effect that, "it is easier to change the dynasty than one's character." On the other hand, we do see evidence of people changing their character throughout history. For instance, in the Bible, it is told that Saul on the road to Damascus falls off his mule and changes from a persecutor of Christians into the person who will become Saint Paul.

By all accounts, Paul experienced a truly transformative change in his whole being as evidenced by his total change in subsequent behavior. Contrast that with the later conversion of Constantine on his way to becoming "Constantine The Great," the first Christian Roman Emperor.

Let's take a moment to study the life of Constantine The Great (Roman Emperor from 306 to 337 AD) before we attempt to determine the degree of internal change he might have experienced through his conversion. According to Lactantius, after the death of his father, one of the three leaders of Rome at the time, Constantine followed his father's policy of tolerance towards Christianity. Although not yet a Christian, he probably judged it a more sensible policy than open persecution and a way to distinguish himself from the "great persecutor" Galerius (Roman Emperor from 305 to 311 AD). As Emperor, Constantine decreed a formal end to persecution, and returned to Christians all they had lost during prior persecutions.

In the civil war with his two rivals claiming the mantle of Emperor, Constantine isolated his main enemy Maxentius by forming an alliance against him with Licinius, the other contender. Constantine forged his alliance with Licinius over the winter of 311–312 AD with the offer of his sister Constantia in marriage. Constantine's advisers and generals cautioned against a preemptive attack on Maxentius, and even his soothsayers recommended against it, stating that the sacrifices had produced unfavorable omens. Constantine, with a certitude that left a deep impression on his soldiers, inspiring them to believe that he had supernatural guidance, ignored all these cautions and early in the spring of 312 AD, he crossed the Cottian Alps with his army.

After a series of sorties, Constantine's army arrived at the final battle field bearing unfamiliar symbols on their standards and shields. According to Lactantius, Constantine was visited by a dream the night before the battle, wherein he was advised "to mark the heavenly sign of God on the shields of his soldiers... by means of a slanted letter X with the top of its head bent round, he marked Christ on their shields." Eusebius describes another version, where, while marching at midday, Constantine, "saw with his own eyes in the heavens a trophy of the cross arising from the light of the sun, carrying the message, *In Hoc Signo Vinces* (with this sign, you will conquer)."

In Eusebius's account, Constantine had a dream the following night, in which Christ appeared with the same heavenly sign, and told him to make a standard, the *labarum*, for his army. Eusebius is vague about when and where these events took place, but it enters his narrative before the war against Maxentius begins. Eusebius describes the sign as *Chi* (X) traversed by *Rho* (P): ☧, a symbol representing the first two letters of the Greek spelling of the word *Christos* or Christ.

Before the battle, Maxentius was confident of victory and enjoyed the support of most of the Roman nobility. He organized his forces, twice the size of Constantine's, in long lines facing the battle plain, with their backs to the river. Constantine deployed his own forces along the whole length of Maxentius' line then ordered his cavalry to charge, and surprisingly, they broke Maxentius' larger ranks of cavalry. Constantine then sent his infantry against Maxentius' infantry, pushing many of them into the Tiber where they were slaughtered and drowned.

The battle was brief as Maxentius' troops were broken before the second charge. Maxentius' Praetorian Guard initially held their position, but broke under the force of Constantine's onslaught, and they fell back to the river. As Maxentius fled with them, he attempted to cross the bridge of boats he had constructed across the Tiber. In a famous scene, he was pushed by the mass of his fleeing soldiers into the river and drowned.

Constantine went on to make Christianity the state religion of the Empire, but he remained unbaptized until near his death. Only when it was clear the end was at hand, did Constantine summoned the bishops of Rome, and told them of his wish to be baptized in the River Jordan where Christ was written to have been baptized. He requested the baptism right away, promising to live a more Christian life should he live through his illness. The bishops, Eusebius records, "performed the sacred ceremonies according to custom." Constantine died soon after at his villa, on the last day of the fifty-day festival of Pentecost directly following *Pascha* (Easter), on 22 May 337 AD.

Difficult as it is to form any accurate interpretation of anyone's inner motivation, I am going to venture that Constantine used his conversion to Christianity as a tactical move. Even a cursory reading of his story reveals that his behavior before and after the "conversion" remained relatively constant. He was a calculating, bold, and unconventional leader, but his vision was simply to return the Empire to a past golden age. He wanted to make Rome great again!

The fact that he allowed the sigil of the Christians to be used by his forces is less than revolutionary when you consider that historians have estimated that perhaps up to one third of his forces were already declared Christians and a large number of the rest were probably sympathizers. And even if "Ancient Alien theorists" believe extraterrestrials WERE involved in making the sign of the cross appear in the sky, his conversion did NOT come out of a vacuum.

So how did Constantine come to his conversion? He most likely thought about it very carefully and weighted the pros and cons. Like everyone else who has ever lived, he let the Parliament of his Mind debate and come to a decision. It was probably not even a close vote.

In theosophy and anthroposophy, the Akashic records are a compendium of all human events, thoughts, words, emotions and intent ever to have occurred. Believed by theosophists to be encoded in a non-physical plane of existence known as the etheric plane, there are many anecdotal accounts of it but no scientific evidence for the existence of such records.

Here is my imagined reading from the Arkashic records of how Constantine made up his mind on this momentous decision…

Delegates from "Gutland" led by the "Pragmatists" voted overwhelmingly to go along with the religion of the new "Son of God" already esteemed by a significant portion of the army. Representatives of "Heartland" led by the "Liberals" strongly supported ending the villainy of the usurper and restoring the glory of Rome! Senators from "Headland" led by "Brian the brain" unanimously voted to do the smart thing. Decision Approved.

How would you make a decision as monumental as the one faced by Constantine as he prepared to battle an army twice the size of his, with greater support, and absolute expectation of victory? You would, of course, let your own Parliament of the Mind debate, and come to a decision. I imagine yours would have better provincial and party names.

Ironically, in historical hindsight it is possible to see that by gaining the patronage of Rome, the nascent Christian Faith won a powerful protector and promoter, but at the cost of losing its diversity and spirit of inquiry. The first to go were religious leaders who had a more favorable view of the Divine Feminine.

At the Council of Nicaea (now Iznik, Bursa province, Turkey), a gathering of Christian bishops convened by Constantine in AD 325, the majority ordained the first ecumenical consensus to represent "all" of Christendom. The minority that refused to go along was quietly executed.

Although previous councils, including the first Council of Jerusalem had met previously to settle matters of dispute, the Council of Nicaea was the beginning of Canon Law, and an endless search for orthodoxy that has ironically only bred an endless heterodoxy that still plagues Christianity to this day.

In trying to understand that your decisions are an amalgamation of different impulses and desires, you must imagine that this complex system of bargaining between different interests groups in your mind is happening in "thought speed" which is not far from light speed. See how fast you just imagined that right now? It is so fast that our internal memory of what we decide is really more like the evening news reporting on what the Great Parliament in DC has decided.

With great introspection and even greater self honestly, you CAN see inside the Parliament Dome and see how the sausage is made. How clean is your mind? What kind of backroom deals and scandals exist in there? Do you really want to know?

The kind of total change of personality exemplified by Saul becoming Paul would be analogous to what we now call "regime change" in the mind of the person. Constantine most likely did not experience this.

Decisions define who we are. As radical as a mental "regime change" might sound, it is also just a decision. Choices and decisions make up the story of every life. Some decisions change the course of a life and can influence the flow of historical events. Sometimes you have time to think about it, to ponder the decision from this way and that, to let the Parliament of your mind argue on and on...

And sometime you have to make an instant decision. To introduce the story of one such decision, let me review a bit of history. On May 7, 1999, during the NATO bombing of Yugoslavia (Operation Allied Force), five JDAM guided bombs hit the People's Republic of China embassy in the Belgrade district of New Belgrade, killing three Chinese reporters and outraging the Chinese public.

According to the U.S. government, they had intended to bomb the nearby Yugoslav Federal Directorate for Supply and Procurement. President Bill Clinton later apologized for the bombing, stating it was accidental. Central Intelligence Agency director George Tenet testified before a congressional committee that the bombing was the only one in the campaign organized and directed by his agency, and they had identified the wrong coordinates for a Yugoslav military target on the same street.

The Chinese government issued a statement on the day of the bombing stating that it was a "barbarous act" and massive protests sprang up around all U.S. diplomatic buildings in the mainland. In Hong Kong, where I was, there were also many protesters surrounding the Consulate compound, but the police prevented anyone from throwing anything. I saw a dozen cops haul away a teenager who ran past the barrier and tried to throw an egg.

News coming out of the mainland quickly got intense, and videos showed the Embassy's façade completely covered in paint and eggs, and every window knocked out by rocks. We get internal cables stating the Consulate in Chengdu has been breached by protestors and SET ON FIRE! Soon, it was clarified that only the residence of the Consul-General was set alight. The protesters never breached the hardline of the main Consulate building.

Thank God, I thought, I know people serving there! Things settled down and I heard my friends from Chengdu were being evacuated to Hong Kong. A couple days later, I run into one of them in the Consulate cafeteria.

PERSONAL INTERLUDE: Hong Kong, May of 1999.

My friend is telling me what really happened. The protests get violent on the third day. Protesters get over the perimeter wall by piling up nearby construction material. Once it is clear the People's Armed Police (PAP) isn't going to intervene right away, everyone is locked down inside the main building. It should have been safe.

The doors are double the strength of the Consulate visa windows so theoretically, it can withstand 30 minutes of automatic gunfire.

Only problem is the Consulate had inadvertently placed a perfect battering ram right outside the door. Right in front of the building is a 20 foot long steel bike rack that is shaped like an inverted T. If 30-40 guys pick that up, and turn it over and start swinging it...

The outer door fails in about 5 minutes.

My friend says for the first time in his career, he had to take out his service pistol and point it at someone with the intention to shoot.

As the protestors cheer their victory over the door and struggle to tear the heavy metal frame away so they can repeat their successful tactic on the inner and only remaining door, my friend says he can see they are mostly just kids, pimply faced teenagers.

He sees someone who looks like a leader telling others what to do. He is coordinating the group to start swinging again. BAM! BAM! BAM! BAM!

It would only be a matter of minutes based on the first door. As the special glass start to crack, my friend thinks he can shoot the leader through the cracked glass.

BAM! BAM! BAM! The front of the bike rack breaks all the way through and gets stuck in the cracked glass. My friend and the leader lock eyes.

My friend cocks back the hammer of his pistol...

The protesters manage to wrench the bike rack loose leaving a basketball size hole in the glass. My friend has a clear shot of the man who had been yelling orders just a moment ago. The protesters stare at my friend. My friend says it seemed like a long time passes in silence and no one moved. Then from outside he can hear other protesters yelling that the PAP is moving in and clearing everyone out.

As the protesters inside the building drop the bike rack and run out, the leader takes one last look at my friend, who still stands frozen pointing his gun, and then leaves.

My friend says it was how calm the other man was that stopped him from shooting. He was never sure if he would have shot or not if the other man had *made a move or if the crowd had been more aggressive in gaining entry. As it was, he retired soon after never having fired a shot in anger during his career.*

We didn't know each other very well and I cannot vouch for everything he told me, but it seemed like he really needed to tell someone. All I can say is that we should all be thankful that the United States of America had a guy like that on the job that day instead of someone less internally balanced who might have made a different decision.

So how does a "regime change" of the mind and subsequent change in character happen? If I am right, the internal precursor to sudden and massive change in the personality must be a revolution in the Parliament of the Mind. In the material world, revolutions tend to happen where there is strong oppression of dissension. It is probably the same way in the world of the mind. If dissident thoughts are kept down by prejudice or blind repetition of dogma, mental pressure is bound to build up (I just had a picture of literal "thought police," thoughts in little police uniforms that chase after "bad" thoughts).

Just as democracy is not the only way countries organize themselves, it is not the only system to organize a mind even though the triune nature of the body almost seem to demand at least a three branch system. In my work as a therapist, I have come across anorexic people who can be described as living in the tyranny of too much head. The "head" idealizes an external image (skinny model) then the "head" dominates the "heart" into wanting that to become reality. The "gut" becomes irrelevant, even expendable and hated.

Let me return to the issue of PTSD for a moment. It is possible to see PTSD is an example of the "heart," as a result of excessive trauma, taking over periodically in revolt and overriding the "head" and "gut." The treatment this point of view suggests is to is to strengthen the body element (the guts of the person) with good food, exercise, and probiotics (it would take another book to expand on this subject sufficiently to cover its importance to human physical health) to re-ground people to their physical reality and prevent the trauma's emotional rip tides from knocking them off their feet.

More importantly, the treatment would also be to strengthen the mental element so it is able to allow the "heart" to have its way when it NEEDS to "re-feel" the trauma again. In a way, it is the "head" needing to cut the experience apart that is creating the stressful results of PTSD by "refusing" to "re-feel" the trauma that the "heart" is DEMANDING. The "head" should be quiet and "go with it."

To reduce the stress of PTSD, the head needs to keep quiet and give the heart what it needs. But why is the heart so stupid as to want to re-feel trauma? The head and the guts just don't' get it. That is because "they" didn't feel it the way the heart did. Excessive trauma can make the whole person (which the emotional aspect will do so the most) identify with the traumatic experiences (please see Chapter 3.1).

When a muscle is overused, it cramps and locks up so you can't do anything else. When an emotion is traumatized, it is overstimulated and will flare up at the least provocation. When a thought is obsessive, there is no room for anything else. PTSD as far as I can tell is a combination of all that and more, but the emotional aspect gets traumatized the most.

It is my contention that as bad as it seems, PTSD can still be cured from… within.

PTSD is of course a much more complicated ailment than I am making it here for illustration of the simple point that we need to have a balanced mental structure. What is the best mental structure?

Freedom with order

In my many years with the diplomatic service, I learned one very important thing about international relations that I was never taught in school. And that is this: **Everyone** thinks they are the "good guy."

How does this translate in the world of the mind? How do you tell a "good" thought from a "bad" one? Seriously, this is perhaps one of the most important things you are going to have to answer for yourself in your entire life. I am NOT going to tell you and possibly no one should.

I will say that, for myself, the best mental structure that I have found and one that I am constantly striving to strengthen is the one that guarantees the maximum amount of freedom and order in my state of mind.

As you can tell from what you have read so far this structure is built on a sound foundation of good communication with the physical, freedom of emotional feeling, and a commitment to mental balance of all available voices. Thought police are for traffic only. Nasty thoughts just die from lack of support.

In one way of looking, achieving this state of mind is already a high plateau. There was a time when I would think "this is as high as I can go and I should be satisfied." Then "try something new" got me into an area I did not see coming.

PERSONAL INTERLUDE: Guangzhou, China. March of 2002.

I am at a diplomatic function hosted by the cultural affairs officer of the Consulate-General. It's a super busy week for us in the Consular Section and I am in no mood to lose another evening to yet another cocktail party, especially as a "filler" American to balance out the mix at one of these things. We get there fashionably late (due to work), my Junior Officer friend was excited, like I was dozens of these ago. We mix and mingle.

I see the guest of honor is some Chinese guy. I work my way over and find out that while the evening is ostensibly to celebrate the visit of leading psychologists from the U.S., the reason they came is to recognize the Chinese gentleman, Professor Heyong Shen. Apparently, he is the first Chinese psychologist to earn the recognition of the International Jungian Association as a Jungian analyst and his university is launching a Ph.D. program this year based on his accreditation. I lean into the small group around Professor Shen and get the Cultural Affairs guy to introduce me. I forget most of what we talked about. It had been a long day and I had not eaten anything, but I wasn't too keen on the finger food at the 3-star hotel. Still, I remember it was an interesting evening and I learned at last the difference between Jungian and Freudian.

A couple days later, the Administrative Officer comes to my office after hours and says, "What is this I hear you want to apply for a Ph.D. program?"

Right, yeah, I did say that, as a joke! There was no way I was going to do my day job and go to school (a doctorate no less) at night.

But with the Admin Guy standing there, I had to say... *"Yeah, that Professor Shen's new program. Can you get me in?"*

"Well, I will process the paperwork the university sent over and see what happens. I'll get back to you later."

A couple weeks later, I had almost forgotten about the conversation when the Admin guy comes back and he is NOT happy. *"The local FAO (Foreign Affairs Office) refused it. They said there is no precedent of allowing credentialed diplomats to have student status at the same time, so I checked with my boss at the Embassy and he says he knows, for a fact, Chinese diplomats are enrolled in US schools, and he's going to talk to the (Foreign Affairs) Ministry about it."*

"It's fine. It was just a spirit of the moment thing, really. Let's just drop it, eh?"

"No! It's a reciprocity thing now! If they won't let you study, we can't let them study. I'll get back to you later."

Two days later, I had hoped the matter would be forgotten when the Admin guy comes back and he is HAPPY. *"They approved it! My boss said once he raised it and mentioned that they would have to pull all their guys out, they agreed right away. You will have to sign some form saying you won't do anything to rile up the kids or something."* He is pretty pleased.

"You can go now." He said with a grin.

Oh, yay?

See what happens when you try something new?

By 2003, I had been an active Baha'i for seven years and was in my second semester of the Ph.D. program. I have had a number of Jungian analysis sessions at this point with my mentors, Professor Shen and his wife Professor Gao, an expert on child psychology. I felt deeply committed to the ideas I was learning and was excited to go to class in the evenings after work. I delved deep into the ideas presented to me – individuation, synchronicity, the personal subconscious, archetypes, the shadow, and ultimately, the collective unconscious. Being part of the program while working as an American diplomat turned out to not be much of an issue after all. The other students respected my situation and never asked for any favors or got into awkward political arguments with me.

A new sense of confidence about the direction I wanted to take in life in general and specific decisions in my personal and professional life came to me. More and more, I found I was able to intuit the answer to difficult and perplexing situations as they came up. As I look back, I recognize that this "ability" was not new, just that I had chosen to ignore it previously.

Intuitive Knowing

There are so many good books on intuition that I am not going to "grind my ax" too much on it here. I have to admit that for me, "intuitive knowing" was not a new experience by 2003, and I could sense there were going to be BIG changes in my life.

Much more subtle than the "gut feeling" that is more clearly felt as a physical thing, and less urgent than the "heart knows what it wants" that is usually more persistent, this is INTUITION.

Let's see what the dictionary has to say about it:

Noun – 1) A direct perception of truth, fact, etc., independent of any reasoning process; immediate apprehension. 2) A fact, truth, etc., perceived in this way. 3) A keen and quick insight. 4) Quality or ability of having such direct perception or quick insight.

Philosophy - An immediate cognition of an object not inferred or determined by a previous cognition of the same object; Any object or truth so discerned; Pure, untaught, non-inferential knowledge.

I can trace the beginning of my "ability" to have strong intuition from a specific moment in 1993.

PERSONAL INTERLUDE: San Francisco, June 4, 1993.

My dad is dying. He has been dying since he had a stroke and never woke up from the surgery that kept him alive and allowed me time to fly back from Japan and spend the last five days of his life by his side. Last night, around

4 am, the nurse warned me, "I've seen this monitor pattern before and you should have all your family here by the morning."

I leave my sister at the room and walk the short distance from the hospital to the house (they just happened to live near it). As I quietly open the door to my mom's room and turn on the light, hoping not to shock her, I am the one surprised to see that she is sitting straight up in bed with her eyes wide open.

"Your dad was just here! He opened the door and said 'I am home'." She blurted out before I could even say a word.

After the whole family gathered at my dad's bedside around 5:00 am, the nurse's experience proved right. The vital signs began to fade and around an hour later, he started to go into cardiac arrest. My mom cried and struggled to lift him, and in a plaintive voice that I had never heard before from the strongest woman I know, she pleaded, "Don't leave me! Please, don't go!"

As if on cue, his vital signs surged back strongly and for a split second, my heart dared to hope. Then inexorably, they began a steep decline. As my brothers pulled my mother aside and comforted her, my sister took my dad's right hand and I took his left. We watched the lines on the monitor fall near the bottom and then went into a flat line. I felt… nothing. I had cried more in the previously few days than all my days before. I was ready to let him move on.

Then I feel something. Something moves up my arm from where I am holding my father's hand. It was not a physical feeling. "It" goes up my arm, over my shoulder and then it seems like "it" flies out the window behind me. I look at the clock, and the arms are straight up and down, 6:00 AM. I walk over to the window and look out. To my right, I see the rising sun, burning away the early mists. To my left, the full moon can still be seen hanging in the morning sky. The two orbs align on the same plane as I stand there and think… "He is free."

A few months after my dad's passing, I am trying to decide whether to accept the first offer for my next posting, Guangzhou, China, after Tokyo. There is a little give and take in the system and it is not uncommon to refuse the first offer and hope for something better to open up later in the transfer cycle. As I am mulling over what to do, one night, I have the most vivid dream I had ever had up to this point in my life…

I am in a white void when suddenly I see a young version of my dad drive up in a red convertible sports car. He gets out and I am so surprised and excited to see him that I run over and bear hug him. I can distinctly remember the solidity of holding him in my arms. He gently pushes me away and without a word point towards a building that appears in the blankness all around us. Reluctantly, I turn away from him and see that he is pointing to a... gas station?

I turn back, but my dad is gone and I am left with a strong sense that this is where he wants me to go. So I go into the gas station and I am amazed to see that inside it is lined with marble and there is a waterfall coming out from what looks like another floor. The incongruity stays with me as I drift into unconsciousness.

Not consciously relating my decision to this particular dream, a few days later I choose to accept the offer to go to Guangzhou. In 1994, the place is nothing like the modern metropolis it becomes just a few years later. At the time, the State Department was paying a "hardship allowance" for postings there. However, the Consulate building is rather nice as it was newly constructed for our use and is part of the 5-Star White Swan Hotel's compound. The first time, I pass through our "rear entrance" passageway to the hotel's pool and into the lobby area I am struck by a powerful sense of déjà vu. The shiny marble floor and walls, the flowing water channels fed by, yep you guessed it, a giant indoor waterfall, coming down from the second floor. A bit later, I am told that our ten floor combined office and residential tower was built on the site of what used to be - the hotel's private gas station.

If you say intuition sounds like "something from nothing," science has an answer for you. A vacuum might seem like empty space, but scientists have discovered a new way to seemingly get something from that nothingness in the form of light. And the finding could ultimately help scientists build incredibly powerful quantum computers or shed light on the earliest moments in the universe's history.

Quantum physics explains that there are limits to how precisely one can know the properties of the most basic units of matter. For instance, one can never absolutely know a particle's position and momentum at the same time. One bizarre consequence of this uncertainty is that a vacuum is never completely empty, but instead buzzes with so-called "virtual particles" that constantly wink into and out of existence. Photons of light can pop in and out of a vacuum.

These virtual particles often appear in pairs that near-instantaneously cancel themselves out. Before they vanish, they can have very real effects on their surroundings and be recorded on detectors. When two mirrors are placed facing each other in a vacuum, more virtual photons can exist around the outside of the mirrors than between them, generating a mysterious force that seemingly pushes the mirrors together.

This phenomenon, predicted in 1948 by the Dutch physicist Hendrick Casimir and known as the Casimir effect, was first seen with mirrors held still. Researchers also predicted a dynamical Casimir effect that can result when the mirrors are moving. Recently quantum physicist Pasi Lähteenmäki at Aalto University in Finland and his colleagues revealed that by varying the speed at which light can travel, they can make light appear from nothing.

The speed of light in a vacuum is constant, according to Einstein's theory of relativity, but its speed passing through any given material depends on a property of that substance known as its index of refraction. By varying a material's index of refraction, researchers can influence the speed at which both real and virtual photons travel within it.

The researchers detected photons that matched predictions from the dynamical Casimir effect. These virtual photons displayed the strange property of quantum entanglement, that is, by measuring the details of one, scientists could in principle know exactly what its counterpart is like, no matter where it is in the universe, a phenomenon Einstein referred to as "spooky action at a distance."

So, nature really does abhor a vacuum because things just pop out of it. It's a long trek from the quantum experiments outlined above to establishing a basis for intuition, but at least, don't say, "You can't get something from nothing."

However, having intuition does not mean you will accept, believe, or act on it. I certainly mostly ignored such feelings even if they did present very clearly in my mind. I would register the memory, but "vote" to go with the much more reliable information that came from much more reliable sources. You know... sources you can see, hear, touch, etc. And if you ignore it, the intuition just fades away.

A few bad mistakes in judgment did not improve my trust of intuition. It was only after another "special dream" in 2003 that I really began to "go with" the feelings of intuitive knowing and to have the courage to base my decisions on them.

PERSONAL INTERLUDE, Guangzhou, China, July of 2003

One night after class, alone in my apartment, I have the following dream...

I am on the ground floor of a large three story house. I am alone. There is a doorway that seems to lead to the basement. I open the door and see a long stairway that seems to lead down into infinite darkness. I feel no fear and in fact feel attracted to go down the stairs. As I descend I cannot see anything to either side of the stairs and the door soon disappears behind me and there is total darkness. I proceed to walk for a bit, but suddenly the stairs tumble away and as I fall the steps turn into razor blades. In the total darkness I can feel, without pain, the sharp edges of the blades slice away my body in a few strokes. Without a body "I" keep descending until a bottom stops me. I then see a dim light in the distance in the form of a human outline. I go towards it and a voice says, "This is your Baha'i body." I enter the glow and it coalesces into the physical body I had before.

Now a light attracts my attention to an opening to my right and I see a large stone staircase heading up. I start to climb it and very quickly find myself in the clouds as the stairs continue to stretch higher into the sky out of sight. I climb for a time and come to a place on the stairway where there is a landing to the left. On the platform stands a man whose right arm ends at the elbow and merges into a sharp sword. He motions for me to stop and asks me, "What is the color of the sun?" I know without pause and answer right away, "the sun has three colors. It is yellow in the morning, white at noon, and orange in the evening." Without expression, he waves his sword and say, "you may pass."

I continue climbing and after a short time I notice a raised stone platform like that under large statues to my right. On the platform reclines a woman dressed in black lace and wearing a black veil. I can see that she is not old but cannot tell much else behind the veil. She lifts her left hand and waved a black scarf for me to stop. I approach and wait for her to speak. In a soft voice, she asks, "who do you love the most, you mother, your wife, or your daughter?" Without hesitation, I answer, "my mother is the past, my wife is the present, my daughter is the future, as I can't live in the past or the future, of course, I love my wife the most." With a slight smirking smile I can see even through the veil, she waves the scarf again for me to move on.

After more steps I see a throne like structure blocking the whole width of the quite wide staircase. For a moment, I noticed more steps beyond though there seemed no way around the throne, but then my attention become focused on the man sitting on the throne. He had the look of a classic Greek or Roman god would be the best shorthand for what I saw. He had a white robe, muscles, was young but mature, and was good looking. And he seemed excited and happy to see me. "You have a question for me?"

"What is the secret to wholeness?" I eagerly ask. The godlike man reaches deep into his robe, as if he is reaching into his chest, and pulls out a glass sphere the size of a bowling ball. "Here it is!" he said with a flourish and hands me the ball with one hand. I gingerly take it with both my hands and I can see inside the glass sphere many twinkling lights. As one part of me noticed that the godlike man had disappeared, the rest of me began to be engrossed in what was inside the sphere and just as I have the idea that each of the lights was a galaxy, I fell into a deep and restful sleep.

The next morning I woke up and unlike almost any other dream I have ever had, the details and images of this dream remained crystal clear and it has to this very day.

In short order, the following things happened, I completed my course work at the university just as I am transferred to a desk job at "Main State" in Washington, D.C. I had reached the mandatory period of time for overseas service and was required to do a domestic tour, my first after 15 years abroad. Working in the bureaucratic environment of Main State helped me make a decision that I had thought about a lot years before that, and in 2005, I resigned from the Foreign Service and moved home to San Francisco.

A year later, I finished my dissertation and went to China for the oral defense. After, I obtained my degree, I remained part time in China and got into some very interesting groups at the forefront of the psychology revolution going on there, and also worked as a therapist, but a couple years later I moved back permanently as my mom's health declined.

I reconnected with my then-future wife and went to China on a whirlwind visit with her to meet her relatives and we got permission from her parents for her hand in marriage. Soon after we got married, we got a cat. That cat liked being outside too much and despite our best efforts, got out and probably ate something bad and died too soon. My wife wanted an English short hair breed as a replacement, but I was reluctant to pay for a pure breed, and insisted we adopt from the shelter as we had before. How we ended up with a pure breed cat from the shelter is too long of a story for here, but trust me when I say, my wife has even stronger intuition then I do.

We are all born with some intuition, or 'sixth sense' with which we can interpret the world beyond our physical senses. Tapping into that and knowing how to use it is a power available to us all. Perhaps it is a combination of the gut feeling, and the heart knows what it wants, as well as intellectual pondering?

However, in my experience, in order to trust it and base your decisions on intuition, it is best to have moved past the lower unity and touched the realm of pure energy in yourself.

The most common forms of intuition are: clairvoyance, clairaudience, clairsentience, and claircognizance.

Clairvoyance (Clear Seeing) is the ability to foresee events, view auras, and discern premonitions. Someone who is strong in this sense may be known to "see through people." They may have prophetic dreams and claim to see auras or spirits. In addition, clairvoyant people are visually creative, and can remember faces and physical details easily.

Clairaudience (Clear Hearing) is the ability to hear voices and messages from the "spiritual plane." One who has a strong clairaudience can discern a deeper meaning behind the words one might speak. They often hear ringing or buzzing in their ears, and are quite sensitive to sounds around them. They are also avid phone talkers and excellent auditory learners.

Clairsentience (Clear Feeling) is the ability to derive feelings in someone. They can often sense trouble or wrongness in another's life. Clairsentient people are prone to goose bumps and inexplicable tingling or other sensations. Often, these people are described as empathetic, tuning into the emotions of someone else and feeling them as well. These people have strong feelings they feel they have no choice but to follow, and they tend to get drained easily in large groups.

Claircognizance (Clear Knowing) is the feeling of "knowing" without any physical evidence or proof. Often the claircognizant will have strong deja vu or receive sudden insights about the past, present or future. They will at times know what someone will say before saying it, and can converse on a wide range of topics even if they have no knowledge base behind them. They are analytical and good at understanding abstract problems.

We probably all have a combination of these gifts, but there is usually one that will stand strongest in each individual. If you perceive such intuitive knowing in your life, I strongly suggest you pay them the attention they deserve.

Chapter Five

$$\text{THE FOURTH STEP}$$

Everything is energy and so are you

So, here we are at the penultimate step before our ONE GIANT LEAP. Let's quickly review. You are not your body. You are not your emotions. You are not your thoughts. When these three aspects of your being work together you have the potential to become (in Jung's term) an *Individuated human* in touch with the subconscious aspect of your life.

I experienced a second type of "Awakening" a few years after completing my Jungian training and thinking myself already solidly on the path of what Jung called individuation ("I gotta be me," was my motto). The first sign of this change in awareness was what I came to think of as my "there is another level" experience.

By 2013, I had been consciously doing the things outlined in the previous chapters for a few years already, and my meditative experiences had settled into a comfort zone. Perhaps because I had already read Bob's books on OBE's and seen so many of Tom's videos on the mechanism behind these kinds of experiences, I developed a strong desire to try to go "out of body" myself. However, it was still just a yearning. My relationship with my mom was much better, and being together with my wife was wonderful. After three years, time, money, opportunity came together, and we were off to Hawaii for a much delayed honeymoon...

PERSONAL INTERLUDE: Honolulu, Hawaii, March of 2014.

My mom's friend is selling her apartment so we get to stay in it for free while it is being listed. There's hardly any furniture and no TV. It is cold for Honolulu but we are having a great time. By day three of our five day visit, we are tired from playing and my wife is taking a nap at noon. I sit in a hardback chair in the living room and try to meditate. It's bright, and noisy, but I remember Tom Campbell saying he could meditate on a dime anywhere.

I sit quietly and turn my attention… within. I let each impression come in, the chair, the air, physical feelings inside the body, emotional feelings moving in and moving on, thoughts, recognition of having thoughts, recognition of attention moving on…

Suddenly with my eyes still closed, I can "see" the room I am in. The light is different, more crystalline, and the perspective is little off, about a couple inches too high, but it is certainly the room. There is a thought of recognition that there is another level of awareness, and then a feeling like that of being let into a giant space and then an emotion of awe came that reminded me of the first time I saw the Grand Canyon with my parents as a teenager. This lasted less than a fraction of a second.

Then I am back in the chair. My eyes are open and without thinking to speak, my mouth opens and I say, "There IS another level!"

In a strange synchronicity, while we are waiting to takeoff from Honolulu to return to San Francisco, the news of Malaysia Airlines Flight 370, the international passenger flight that disappeared on 8 March 2014 while flying from Kuala Lumpur International to Beijing, "disappearing" hit the screens. I tried months later to use remote viewing to get more information on what happened and could not see anything conclusive, but I did "see" people who looked like passengers in a detention facility.

As I practiced the lifestyle and mindset I write about in the earlier chapters, a subtle change occurred in my psyche. I could "see" inside the Parliament of my mind. With practice, my inner attention could easily keep up with all the deal making and high oratory going on in there.

Before long, I realized – it's all kabuki theater! My life was actually ruled by a hidden "Emperor" who had final say on every decision that came out of the Parliament Dome. The Emperor's name is "I AM," and it is "he" that energetically held the reins of power in this here person. I realized on a deep level that all the discussions and contemplations of this or that psychological theory that I had ever held in my mind was like a show before the Emperor who had the decision on what to "accept or not accept" as part of "I AM."

If someone's "lesser unity" was not already in harmony, it would be unlikely that their energetic aspect could be perceived consciously at all, and if it could, it would likely only be as an *"Enfant terrible."* The energy "Emperor" would still be really calling the shots, but the conscious personality would hardly know it.

It is my experience that when the "lesser unity" of the three lower aspect of human existence are in working harmoniously together, intuition and the like will appear. And it is from one's energy aspect that the intuition comes. This is because only with a firm "lesser unity," the influence of the least substantial aspect of being human, the energy aspect of existence will exert itself. For me, until the lower aspects were strongly attached together in my conscious sense of self, I found it difficult to even perceive "I AM", much less contemplate moving beyond it.

From this point on my discussion is going to be much more personal. When I was writing about the aspects of the human being that make up what I call the "lesser unity," I was confident that what I am communicating are things that are common to everybody. However, as I begin to write about an aspect of inner experience that feels beyond personal experience, I become unsure if anyone else will necessarily have this kind of experience in a similar way…

As I write this, I begin to wonder if "I AM" was symbolized and intimated by the godlike man from my dream in 2003, still so clear in my mind after so many years, blocking the path upwards to even higher domains…

Around the time I was able to perceive "I AM" in myself, my wife and I began having deep discussions on the nature of reality and I sought to understand her interpretation of the Buddhist texts that she had read. My classical Chinese being not adequate, I had to take her word for what was written. In the years of marriage up to that time, we had only argued twice, both due to minor misunderstandings. This time, we actually had a heated argument at one point. What was it in her understanding of the nature of reality that I had so much resistance to?

In my experience, the preparations I had made on the three lower levels of being human did much to bring on what happened next, but the awareness of "I AM" in myself and the argument with my wife was what pushed it out...

PERSONA INTERLUDE: San Francisco, November 12th, 2014.

I am taking a shower. My mind is blank as I focus on shampooing and not getting any in my eye.

Suddenly I am laughing out loud, there is a mental lapse as the first thought is, "what is so funny?"

I am filled with the emotion of suddenly being let in on a cosmic joke... Now THAT is funny!

Even the "Emperor" is laughing!?!

EVERYTHING IS ENERGY AND SO AM I...

The word Satori (悟り?) (Chinese: 悟; Korean: 오 o; Vietnamese: ngộ) is a Japanese Buddhist term for awakening, "comprehension; understanding." It is derived from the Japanese verb satoru.

In the Zen Buddhist tradition, satori refers to the experience of kenshō, "seeing into one's true nature." Ken means seeing, shō means nature or essence.

Satori and kenshō are commonly translated as enlightenment, a word that is also used to translate bodhi, prajna and Buddhahood.

Usually, the student's mind must be prepared by rigorous study, with the use of koans, and the practice of meditation to concentrate the mind, under the guidance of a teacher.

Koans are short anecdotes of verbal exchanges between teachers and students, typically of the Song dynasty, dealing with Buddhist teachings. The Rinzai-school utilizes classic collections of koans such as the Gateless Gate.

The Gateless Gate was assembled by the early 13th-century Chinese Zen master Wumen Hui-k'ai (無門慧開). Wumen struggled for six years with a single koan, assigned to him by Yuelin Shiguan (月林師觀; Japanese: Gatsurin Shikan) (1143–1217), before attaining kenshō.

After his understanding had been confirmed by Yuelin, Wumen wrote the following enlightenment poem:

A thunderclap under the clear blue sky
All beings on earth open their eyes;
Everything under heaven bows together;
Mount Sumeru leaps up and dances.

Had I experienced Satori?

All I can say is I now KNOW everything is energy and so are you and me.

And I wrote this…

Touch the outer moon, one small step
Grasp the Inner Sun
One Giant Leap

There is an aspect of being human that cannot be named. You can't think it, you can't imagine it. You even can't dream it. You are ALREADY it. It is ALREADY you. Don't try to name it. Don't try to feel it. Try to let it BE through you.

You already KNOW what to do. Take good care of your body. Feel what you feel. Reclaim your power. Free your mind. Cultivate and refine your life energies, and point your life direction in the direction of what Jung called your Self. All that remains is to actually walk the path…

My concept of "energy" is not so divergent from the Chinese quality of "qi" and the Hindu concept of "prana" (or even *The Force* as described in the Star Wars movie franchise) that I need to expand on it too much here. I find the teachings of both of these traditions to be exceptionally rich mines of useful information and highly recommend you spend some time researching both of them.

Now that we are at the "energy" aspect portion of the book, let's review what mainstream science has to say on the matter. Most high school students are now taught that matter equals energy and Einstein worked out how and gave us atomic weapons. E=MC squared. Any non-physics majors know what that actually means? If you say, yes, and it means "all matter is just cooled down energy, like steam into water," then that's pretty much what I heard in high school as well.

Now, what does it MEAN? If matter is condensed energy then what is energy and where did THAT come from? For non-physics majors (I am one), here is a quick review of what MOST physicists today think about where the universe came from.

Billions of years ago, around 1.38 billion by their estimate, everything in the universe was pure energy. This energy was so condensed that what we now see as the "universe" was compacted into a point so small, that it is smaller than the smallest particle that the scientists at CERN (derived from the French name *Conseil Européen pour la Recherche Nucléaire*, it is a European research organization that operates the largest particle physics laboratory in the world) have ever found despite spending close to 1.5 trillion dollars.

While the scientific community was once divided between supporters of two different expanding universe theories, the Big Bang and the Steady State theories, in 1964 cosmic microwave background radiation was discovered and provided what was seen as crucial evidence in favor of the Big Bang model. This "creation" of the universe from its infinitesimal beginning through a "Big Bang" is now generally held to be true by the majority of cosmologists. However, there are "dissident" voices and the one I think everyone needs to hear is physicist Thomas Campbell.

Tom Campbell began researching altered states of consciousness with Bob Monroe at Monroe Laboratories in the early 1970s where he and a few others were instrumental in getting Monroe's laboratory for the study of consciousness up and running. These early drug-free consciousness pioneers helped design experiments, developed the technology for creating specific altered states, and were the main subjects of study (guinea pigs) all at the same time. Tom has been experimenting with, and exploring the subjective and objective mind ever since. For the past thirty years, he has been focused on scientifically exploring the properties, boundaries, and abilities of consciousness.

During that same time period, he has excelled as a working scientist, a professional physicist dedicated to pushing back the frontiers of cutting edge technology, large-system simulation, technology development and integration, and complex system vulnerability and risk analysis.

Tom is the "TC (physicist)" described in Bob Monroe's second book Far Journeys and has been a serious explorer of the frontiers of reality, mind, consciousness, and psychic phenomena since the early 1970s. His trilogy "My Big TOE (Theory of Everything) is a model of existence and reality that is based directly on Tom's scientific research and firsthand experience. It represents the results and conclusions of thirty years of careful scientific exploration of the boundaries and contents of reality from both the physical and metaphysical viewpoints.

In my opinion, Tom has made every effort to approach his explorations without bias or preconceived notions. There is no belief system, dogma, creed, or unusual assumptions at the root of his Big TOE. By demanding high quality repeatable, empirical, evidential data to separate what's real (exists independently and externally) from what's imaginary or illusory; Tom has scientifically derived his general model of reality.

In Tom's view, material reality is a virtual reality run in an information system that was created to allow individuated units of consciousness (IUOC) to experience this virtual reality using "avatars" to "live" inside this reality. The IUOC would be equivalent to one's "being level" that I write about. Human consciousness existing as free will awareness units (the avatars) can learn to grow through choices made in this reality BECAUSE it IS physical. Physical means consequences. If you didn't have a body, a lot of things would not matter to you and what you did or didn't do would have almost no chance to affect the "essential" you. With physicality comes choice with consequence.

To fully appreciate the intricately arrived at conclusions in My Big TOE, you need to read it yourself. My wife and I met Tom for the first time in Los Angeles in 2016, and that meeting inspired me to write One Giant Leap.

Tom also inspired this final five part metaphor of the essential human being. The body is the computer, it sets the limit on a lot of your abilities and if it breaks down, you lose abilities. The emotions are your display and control unit, it is how you perceive and interact. Your thoughts are all the software that runs everything, and these can be changed (or infected). Your energy is the electricity that makes it all run. And your being level is the computer engineer.

Cultivating and refining life energy

When people talk about life energy, the topic of ghosts almost always comes up. It seems to be an obvious question no matter how you look at it unless you are a total materialist, then ghosts are just unreal fantasy figures for you. What happens to the soul, the immortal spirit, etheric body, whatever name you give it, when a person "gives up the ghost" as the saying goes? All cultures have the concept of the ghost. Although generally considered an object of fear, does it not also offer assurance of consciousness remaining intact beyond physical death?

There are already so many other books on this subject, I am going to limit my remarks to this: We cannot conclusively say what ghosts are, but their prevalence across time, cultures, and places leads me to believe that there must be a real non-material explanation behind people's experience with the phenomenon.

In Chapter Three, I described my encounter with a ghostly being that might have been a dream in Shenzhen, but now I will share an experience that was definitely not a dream...

PERSONAL INTERLUDE: Taipei, Taiwan, July of 1991.

It was weird "resigning" as soon as I joined the State Department to work as a "non-diplomat" in Taiwan, but the Institute has the feel of an Embassy and I even found an old stamp in my desk that read American Embassy Taipei, Republic of China. On my first day, I met a great guy working here as a summer intern on his last year before law school. One Saturday night we had been out dancing with some of the female interns and the two of us shared a cab with the one girl who also lived on Yangming Mountain just outside the city.

It was July and very warm and we were all tired. It must have been around 2:00 am. The girl lived off the main road, and at her instruction, the taxi turned onto a narrow unlit lane. It was a steep climb with a high cliff wall on one side and a deep ravine on the other, but it was wide enough that the taxi comfortably drove up with room to spare. After a few minutes, we drove up to the house, and to my surprise hidden way up here on the side of the mountain was an American style mini-mansion with what must have been quite the view during the day. I woke from my daze and said "good night."

On the way down, I recalled that she had told us that her dad was a military contractor who married a local Taiwanese and retired here. My buddy and I are both more awake now and then all of a sudden, we are both fully awake. In fact, I dare say we were both RAPT by what we saw in the headlights of the taxi as it slowly went back down the side road that we had just come up.

What can I say? It was a "classic" Chinese ghost!

There was the long black hair that hung straight down over a green hued expressionless face. Check. A thin body clothed in a plain white gown. Check. No visible feet under the helm of her gown AND her whole body is glowing. Check and check!

Before we could react, say, or even really think or, in my case, feel anything. The driver swerves around "her" and keeps driving maintaining the same speed.

As one, my friend and I spin around in the backseat and see that "she" has turned around to look back at us. Now, my mind catches up and the first thought is - That IS a ghost. The second thought is - Why am I not more scared? The third thought is - I should say something.

I turn and say to my friend, "looks like she likes you and wants to follow you home."

Fourth thought is - why would I say that?

My friend looks at me with such a look of horror that I instantly regretted the words that came out of my mouth. "Don't say that!" He screamed.

We turned to look again and the "girl" was still glowing though no light was shining on "her."

Slowly "she" receded into the distance as the taxi kept driving down the road. Assured that, whatever it was, was not following us, I asked the driver in Mandarin, "ni kan jian NE GE gui la ma?" (Did you see THAT ghost?)

He says nothing. Not a word. On the way out of the city, he was quite chatty, but now? Nope.

My friend and I compared notes in English. Black hair, long, straight down, young girl's deadpan face, green, and yep, glowing!

I would have gone on, but he made me stop. But there could be no question about it... we saw the same whatever it was.

My friend catches a bad cold after that and missed a couple days of work. When we see the girl that lived on the side of the mountain, she filled us in. Apparently, a few years back, a minibus went over the cliff there and they could not recover all of the bodies, a young woman was never found. And it was Ghost Month in Taiwan when the "hungry dead" (the deceased with unrequited wishes especially those not properly buried who come out and look for their family home) need to be placated with offerings of ceremonial food and incense.

I want to publicly apologize to my buddy for saying what I did and scaring him that night. However, years later, after much reflection two things were revealed to me. The first came easily when I reflected that he was on the side of the taxi that faced "her" when we passed and he screened me from seeing any more than what I did (what did he see?). The second came much later after a deeper review of the event in meditative remembering.

On some level, I did sense that she liked him and would like to follow him home. It would not be to his home, his physical residence. "Home" is where wandering spirits stop wandering. What I remembered was the look of sadness and deep sense of isolation on her face. At that time of my initial meditative remembering, I had no idea what else there was to do. At the time the event took place we were too young to know any better than just be scared.

Many years later, after I had learned much more about the energetic nature of reality, I did return and pay a visit to this wandering spirit and give her a helping hand, but that is a story for another time…

After that "camp fire ghost story," let's orientate back to the topic of this book, how YOU can make One Giant Leap past the energy level, the least physical aspect of human existence, and into the final, completely non-physical aspect of human existence. But well before anyone can have much success contacting their "being level," they will need to really cultivate and refine their life energies.

So before we proceed to the conclusion of this book, I want to share my experience with "qigong." Qigong (Chinese: 氣功; pinyin: qìgōng, literal translation: life energy cultivation) is a holistic system of coordinated body posture and movement, breathing, and meditation used for health, spirituality, and martial arts training. With roots in Chinese medicine, philosophy, and martial arts, qigong is traditionally viewed as a practice to cultivate and balance one's qi - life energy.

According to Taoist, Buddhist, and Confucian philosophy, qigong allows access to higher realms of awareness, awakens one's "true nature," and helps develop human potential. Growing up I was familiar with popular depictions of qigong in martial arts stories, and from my brother's description of it via what he learned from his tàijí quán (literal translation Supreme Ultimate Boxing) teacher. What I learned from practicing qigong was how to cultivate and refine my life energies.

PERSONAL INTERLUDE: Guangzhou, China. August of 1995.

Finally, I have officers who report to me. From the start, we have local staff to supervise, but now I get to boss Americans around! On the visa line one morning, one of the Junior Officers I supervised comes over and says, "There is a weird guy at window 3. His documents say he is a government UFO researcher. That can't be real, right? And I can't understand a thing he is saying."

"That's funny. I'll take care of it, have him sit and I will call him up in a sec."

"Good morning, Mr. Tiger (not his real name)?" I say in Mandarin as it's the default dialect we use even though we are in the linguistic heartland of Cantonese.

"Nee How," He smiles with blackened teeth from years of smoking and tea, I am guessing.

His Mandarin is worse than the white JO, no wonder they could not communicate.

I switch to Cantonese and he opens up like a flower. He wants to go to Puerto Rico to visit his daughter who married and moved there a few years ago and now is having their first child. He goes on about how long they have not seen each other, how much he misses her, and wants to see his grandson...

An aside about the U.S. Non-Immigrant Visa, the officer is tasked by Immigration Law to determine if the applicant has enough ties to his/her home country that they can show they have overcome the legal "presumption" (the key word) of their intent to immigrate instead of non-immigrate.

In Guangzhou in 1995, to overcome that presumption was hard and the refusal rate hovered around 80 percent. People come in hopeful, 4 out 5 leave dejected and out the application fee. Mr. Tiger, however, was able to overcome that presumption.

If I was not the boss and free to spend as much time as I wanted to talk to him, if I did not speak Cantonese, and if he did not trust me... I doubt he would have told me what he did.

We used to joke among ourselves that there was a book in all the weird applicants and fraud we saw in China! And one learns not to be gullible quickly on "the line." Despite my natural sympathies as an immigrant from the region myself, the law is clear, the intent to immigrate is presumed. So with family that he "missed so much" settled down in Puerto Rico, what's to keep grandpa from never leaving?

I am feeling nice that morning and let him ramble while I look over his papers...

He is a director at some kind of Chinese NGO to study UFOs? The address is in Beijing, so what is he doing here? OK, enough of this!

Confession: With great power can come... great ego! Not always but often enough that you see a lot of that, right? Well, as visa chief at a place with an 80% refusal rate, I had the power of the gate keeper. I also speak like a native, so I know what's what, and I am not going to let this guy "pull the wool" over my eyes.

"Okay, that's enough." I put the papers back in order while I prepare my line of questioning in my mind.

"When's that white ghost coming back?" He injects.

"White person," I say and shoot him a look.

"White person, white person," he says sheepishly.

On cue, the JO comes back and looks over my shoulder. "So, is this guy for real?"

"Not sure yet, but he's not your typical fraud profile either."

"Wei, Shien Sheng, ni lao ban zai ma, wuo bu gen zhong guo ren shuo (Hey, Mister, is your boss around, I don't want to talk to this Chinese guy)." Tiger yells to the JO behind me.

"Is he saying he wants to talk to my boss?" He looks at me quizzically. I smile and nod.

"He is my boss! I mean, Ta Shi Wuo Lao Ban!" The JO yells back through the reinforced glass. "Wuo Lao Ban!" he says, pointing at me.

Tiger looks at me. Suddenly it dawns on him that the white ghost didn't dump him on some local flunky. He HAD been speaking to "the boss."

The JO and I laugh out loud and any tension is released. I tell everyone to go to lunch as the rest of the waiting room has cleared out. I wasn't that hungry and had plans for a big dinner, so I stayed and found out all I could about Mr. Tiger through the interview window…

It turns out the UFO thing in Beijing is more like a club even though it is full of highly respected scientists and academics and enjoys some degree of official support. He doesn't live in there, just once a year or so goes there. His income is not from this. He can't show any type of income because it is all in cash. It is all in cash because he is a qigong master who treats rich people and members of the government. It is not officially sanctioned work, but everyone knows that all the top leaders have their own personal qigong masters. He tells me about how he got started and some of the qi "experiments" he has seen and been involved in…

Well, extraordinary claims must come with some pretty extraordinary evidence, right? And no time like the present…

So I say to him, "can you 'fa qi' (send energy) through the window right now?"

"I can try..." He looks around to check that the waiting room is empty then he steps back a couple steps and strikes what we used to call the "invisible chair" stance as kids in Hong Kong.

Gently, he puts one palm out while keeping the other at the waist. He extends the palm towards me, fingers up and just holds it there.

Suddenly, I feel like someone turned on a faucet and water is running over me from the direction of his hand. I am a little surprised, but given we had been building up to this moment for almost an hour I would have been disappointed if nothing happened.

I try to see how I could test the feeling to see if I am just imagining it...

Then it began to move!

As I watched his hand move up and down, a good five feet away and blocked by reinforced bullet proof glass that can withstand 15 minutes of machine gun fire, the feeling of flowing water matched his movement. Suddenly, he emitted a huge, and I mean huge, burp, then another and another, and another... So much gas, I was surprised he didn't deflate.

"You have a lot of 'yin' energy in you right now." Tiger straightens up and composes himself.

"I believe you."

I think I found MY qigong master.

In the months that followed I did become Tiger's "disciple," and got to know his extended family. I will keep his real name private because he was told not to talk about a lot of the stuff he told me, and I am probably considered an "American spy" just because of my former job by some circles.

Although Tiger's family are all in Puerto Rico (legally immigrated) now, last I heard he had returned to China to continue working. Apparently it pays pretty well if you really can heal with qigong.

I hesitate to say this, but within a very short time, I saw contradictions within his understanding of qi. I kept my thoughts to myself out of respect for the persecution he suffered during the Cultural Revolution for those views and my own relative inexperience. His basic qi strengthening techniques were great and came down pretty much unchanged from the Shaolin tradition.

Thank you, Tiger for giving me a good foundation.

As I think about it now, the chance meeting with Tiger and the various qigong training (when my enthusiasm was highest) that I worked on before the "encounter" in that Shenzhen hotel room, just a few months later, probably prepared me in ways that I did not appreciate at the time. Otherwise, the encounter might have had a different outcome.

Mr. Tiger was the most interesting person to ever come across my visa window... Well, there were others, but those would be still classified...

Let's start with the basics, shall we. The first thing the monks have you do if you were lucky enough to train at the Shaolin temple is to learn morning calisthenics. Like everything, you start with the foundation...

This is what I do...

Every morning I get up, I drink some water and do a set of stretches based on the Ba Duan Jin qigong (八段錦) exercises. Ba Duan Jin, variously translated as Eight Pieces of Brocade, Eight-Section Brocade, Eight Silken Movements or Eight Silk Weaving, the name of the form generally refers to how the eight individual movements of the form characterize and impart a silken quality (like that of a piece of brocade) to the body and its energies.

One of the most common forms of Chinese qigong used as exercise, Ba Duan Jin is primarily designated as a form of medical qigong meant to improve health. This is in contrast to religious or martial forms of qigong. However, this categorization does not preclude the form's use as a prelude to deeper meditation or as a martial arts supplementary exercise.

This exercise is mentioned in several encyclopedias originating from the Song Dynasty. The Pivot of the Way (Dao Shi, c. 1150) describes an archaic form of this qigong. The Ten Compilations on Cultivating Perfection (Xiuzhen shi-shu, c. 1300) features illustrations of all eight movements. The same work assigns the creation of this exercise to two of the Eight Immortals, namely Zhongli Quan and Lü Dongbin.

Nineteenth century sources attribute the style to semi-legendary Chinese folk hero General Yue Fei, and describe it as being created as a form of exercise for his soldiers. The legend states he taught the exercise to his men to help keep their bodies strong and well-prepared for battle, and Yue is mention as a lineage master in the second preface of the "Sinew Changing Classic" manual (1624) as the creator of Ba Duan Jin qigong.

The exercises as a whole are broken down into eight separate movements with each to be done eight times. Each is focused on a different physical area and qi meridian. The Ba Duan Jin traditionally contains both a standing and seated set of eight postures each, but in the modern era, the standing version is by far the most widely practiced, and is the one I will outline here.

The particular order in which the eight pieces are executed sometimes varies, with the following order being the most common.

Ba Duan Jin Qigong

Two Hands Hold up the Heavens

This move is said to stimulate the "Triple Warmer" meridian. It consists of an upward movement of the hands, which are loosely joined and travel up the center of the body.

Commentary: Make sure you breathe in fully to start each movement, slowly exhale as you move to the stretched position then breathe in to return to start position. Exhale fully as you reach the fully stretched out position of each move. Start to inhale as you begin to return to start and fully inhale as you rest back in start position.

Time the movements' speed to the time of your breathing. Avoid rushing through these movements. If you do, there will little or no "qigong" quality to doing them, simply muscle movements. The thoughtful connection of the breath to movement to the emotional quality of the "doing" is all one "thing." If you do this for health, it is that. If you do it with the feeling it is for health and happiness, it is that. If you do it with the thought it is for health, happiness, and it is an ancient Chinese system of esoteric movements that might give you mystical powers?

This not like capturing Pokemon!

However, if you think this is for health, happiness, and a good experiment to see what it will do for your mind-heart-body integration, then I congratulate you!!

Drawing the Bow to Shoot the Eagle

While in a lower horse stance, the practitioner imitates the action of drawing a bow to either side. It is said to exercise the waist area, focusing on the kidneys and spleen.

Commentary: It is fun to imagine you are really shooting an arrow while doing this one. "Shoot" your attention with each movement.

You can also do these with your eye closed once you get good and have established your balance.

More adventurous types can try listening to binaural sound while doing these movements.

I found the combination of the left/right aspect of the physical movements seem to help with the synchronization of the left and right brain hemispheres that binaural tones have been proven to affect.

Separate Heaven and Earth

This resembles a version of the first piece with the hands pressing in opposite directions, one up and one down. A smooth motion in which the hands switch positions is the main action, and it is said to especially stimulate the stomach.

Commentary: There are two ways (four actually) to do this one. You can point your fingers in or out as you do the pressing movement. It stretches difference tendons in the hands and arms.

Wise Owl Gazes Back

This is a stretch of the neck to the left and the right in an alternating fashion.

Commentary: If you have neck pain, start gently with this one, do the movement slower than the others and breathe more deeply. Over time, it will provide great relaxation of any tightness in the area.

Sway the Head and Shake the Tail

This is said to regulate the function of the heart and lungs. Its primary aim is to remove excess heat (xin huo) from the heart. Xin huo is also associated with heart fire in traditional Chinese medicine. In performing this piece, the practitioner squats in a low horse stance, places the hands on thighs with the elbows facing out and twists to glance backwards on each side.

Commentary: This is one of the more difficult movements to do well. If you have a "tight" heart or a lot of "fire" in your heart, you might find this movement particularly hard to do at first. The more reason to do it nice and slow, really breathe into it… Feel the tightness, where is it, what is that physical feeling telling you emotionally? How do you feel emotionally as you repeat the movement more deeply each time? Do you feel any different as you do Ba Duan Jin (with feeling) over the coming days, weeks, months…?

Two Hands Hold the Feet to Strengthen the Kidneys and Waist

This involves a stretch upwards followed by a forward bend and a holding of the toes.

Commentary: The classic up down stretch. However, here the movement is slow and the point is not so much the physical stretching but to feel each direction of flow as you traverse the full reach of your body. At the end of the movement you can hold for a moment before you inhale to go back to start.

Clench the Fists and Glare Fiercely

This resembles the second piece, and is largely a punching movement either to the sides or forward while in horse stance. This, which is the most external of the pieces, is aimed at increasing general vitality and muscular strength.

Commentary: This is the only movement in Ba Duan Jin that is clearly martial. Squat and punch is what it looks like on the physical level. Emotionally, it is "reclaiming your power" personified.

Bouncing on the Toes

This is a push upward from the toes with a small rocking motion on landing. The gentle shaking vibrations of this piece is said to "smooth out" the qi after practice of the preceding seven pieces.

Commentary: I altered this to a leaping off the ground movement for myself after my leg muscles became stronger and I turned the "smoothing out" into another movement all together. Remember, it is not that there is a "right" and a "wrong" way to do the work of growing up rather it is more about "do or do not."

For a very good video presentation of these forms, I can suggest Jake Mace watching him do them on YouTube.

According to his profile, he is an environmentalist, vegan, urban farmer and gardener, energy conservationist, animal and human rights activist. His mission statement is: *Inspiring people and raising awareness for Environmental, Human and Animal, and Energy causes by leading workshops, leading seminars, producing videos, and living an example of the life one teaches.*

Jakes lives this example by adopting animals, growing all the food for his family at his home in Tempe Arizona, eating and living a vegan lifestyle, producing all energy for his family through 28 Solar Panels on his home, and driving a "Zero Emission" electric vehicle. He is currently applying to adopt his first child internationally with his wife Pamela.

You can find his many videos, including the ones on Ba Duan Jin at two YouTube channels

1. YouTube.com/ShaolinCenter
2. YouTube.com/OrderTaiChi

PERSONAL INTERLUDE: Guangzhou, China. July of 1996.

Hong Kong is reverting to Chinese control in less than a year! It's the subject on everyone's mind down the river, but it is too hot in Guangzhou for me to care too much. I am sitting by the pool with Tiger watching his granddaughter from his son play in the pool. Her parents are laughing and chasing her around the shallow end. I signed them all in with my hotel card and ordered everyone drinks.

Oh, look who I see. "Hey! Come on over!" It's the JO that interviewed Tiger.

I remind each of them who the other is and they smile in recognition.

A mischievous idea suddenly enters my mind. "Remember you said you weren't sure if qigong was real? Let's try something."

In Cantonese, I say to Tiger, "Hey, sifu, do your medical scan on him."

"Oh my God... What is that! WHAT IS THAT!!"

There are many variations on these forms and many other forms of qigong and many other methods to cultivate and refine one's energies. The most important thing is to find the practice that resonate with you and DO it. Cultivating and refining one's energy is a long term project. It takes human beings 18 years to reach (legal) physical maturity, how many more years to reach emotional and intellectual maturity? If you begin to invest in perceiving, cultivating and refining your energies today, how long before you can expect the first signs of maturation?

I learned this very useful set of qigong exercises from Tiger and practiced it on and off for years. He also taught me other stuff and told me a lot of interesting if unverifiable stories...

For the last ten years, I have done these qigong exercises EVERY morning unless due to some exigent circumstance and I can't. And I have developed the confidence to invent my own moves and trust my feelings when it comes to the cultivation of my energy. And THAT has made all the difference. Now instead of looking for ways to refine my energies in a book or from a teacher exclusively (external), I also look... within.

I altered the eight forms into twelve in my practice and do each twelve times instead of eight. You can find something that works for you and alter it to suit you, but you must do it consistently and do it with all you've got, physically involved, emotionally involved and mindfully involved too.

At night before bed, I regularly do a set of yoga inspired light stretches to limit any body tightness that would intrude into my sleep. I try to not to drink too much water to limit the chance of needing to get up. However, I do leave a thermos to always have some warm water in case my mouth gets too dry. All of this is to increase and improve the chances of entering and maintaining contact with the non-material aspect of the human being during my transition into the modes of consciousness we collectively call "sleep."

A full exposition of even just some of the realms I have entered through lucid dreaming and more clearly OBE's since the breakthrough I had with the Inner Sun practice, described a little later, would require more space than I can afford here.

As you approach and leap into non-physical reality, it is going to be different than physical reality in many ways. Some of the things you might experience will be similar to things you have heard of like OBE, remote viewing, prophetic dreams, etc. These "abilities" sometimes become an attraction for some and they look at acquiring these "abilities" as the reason to do what is called called for here.

That would be a MISTAKE.

That approach puts the path of creation in reverse. You acquire objects. You feel emotions. You generate thoughts. You intuit. Raising the quality of the consciousness is what is allowing these "abilities" to become part of you.

The idea you want to get them (like capturing Pokemon) so you try to raise your consciousness is going to get in the way.

If you picture a spectrum of consciousness in someone, the appearance of these "abilities" would probably indicate that the person is now standing at the threshold of a higher intensity level.

If you are ready, from this point, one of things one can do is to consciously intend to have an OBE. Going "out of body" will give you many more opportunities to learn, but it is not required. And, you DON'T have to try to do it to make One Giant Leap work. The leap is not to get "out of body," it is to a deeper (higher) aspect of YOU.

If you feel yourself becoming more integrated, and able to handle provocations that you could not before, in other words, more loving, keep doing whatever you are doing. The POINT is not to go out of body or "achieve" any level of anything. LOVE is the goal and the answer. Become more loving and you are on the right path.

If you do try to go "out of body" and nothing happens then try something else.

If you do try to go "out of body" and something happens, don't be scared.

There are three rules that I learned from Tom Campbell for OBEs.

These three rules have protected and guided me in all my travels.

I re-phrased them to give them more personal meaning to me.

I share them with you here and hope they can help you.

"Out of body" is not really what is happening at all.

All that you experience in this state is… within.

Memorize these three rules before you leap.

The Three Rule of Giant Leaping…

RULE NUMBER ONE:
FEAR WILL MAKE IT BAD EVEN IF IT ISN'T.

RULE NUMBER TWO:
EGO WILL ONLY SEE WHAT IT WANTS TO SEE.

RULE NUMBER THREE:
THINGS YOU BELIEVE BUT DON'T KNOW WILL TRAP YOU.

Rules to leap by if I say so myself! Then when you are ready…

Conclusion

ONE GIANT LEAP

A leap of faith has been called "An empty handed jump into nothing." In a way, that is what I am asking you to do now. Once you have come to your own conclusion that the facts, images, and concepts I have presented to you in the preceding chapters are indeed true. You can try for yourself the difference in attitude it makes to hold a proper understanding of the nature of human existence in mind as much as possible during your waking hours. Remember, you are not your body, you are not your emotions, and you are not your thoughts. You share your energy with all living things. You are part of a holistic universe growing up together.

Let me expand from a psychologist's perspective what I earlier wrote from a diplomat's point of view. "Everyone thinks they are the good guy." A good diplomat recognizes that each side is self-interested, only from a different perspective and in doing so perceive what would serve their interest as well as the antagonist. A good psychologist would add that however one sees oneself as being internally (deep down) forces one to assume that others are the same way deep down.

A thief cannot trust. An angel sees only angels in everyone deep down.

But everyone needs to acknowledge that however we see ourselves now is transitional and not the inevitable destination of all humanity just because we are the way we are now. Just because you are not a certain way, does not mean others are not that way already, or that you can never be that way. Everyone CAN grow up.

As you practice eating the right amount of food, the right kinds of foods, you can try new ways to use the attention you spend on physical things (like buying stuff you don't need, watching mindless shows, or gossiping with friends) on more emotionally satisfying things. By making art in some way, appreciating nature, or just listening to music you can find good ways to devote your attention to strengthening your emotional life. If you do have emotional issues that require professional help, you can find it.

Reclaiming your emotional power will allow you to use your full rational mind, combining all aspects of your lesser unity. A strong presence of mind and internal sense of harmony can now be yours. As you learn to map your individuated path through the reality that you can now see is energetically real and not materially real, you can experience new trust in your sense of intuition.

Once you arrive at this point, if not long before, you MUST meditate to go even further.

Fortunately, meditation is becoming widely acknowledged as beneficial and much information is publicly available. For our purpose here, just remember that all meditation techniques are ways to train the mind to induce a specific mode of consciousness.

Research on the body's stress signals show how meditation may help the body respond to stressful situations. According to a new study that took a rigorous look at how the practice affects people's physiology when they're under pressure in which people with anxiety disorder took an eight-week course in mindfulness meditation the results were obvious. In the study, the subjects learned to focus on the present moment and accept difficult thoughts or feelings. After completing the course, the participants showed reduced levels of stress hormones and markers of inflammation during a stressful event, compared with how their bodies reacted before the course.

Importantly, the study also involved a comparison group of people who took a course in stress management that did not involve meditation.

These participants did not show a similar reduction in their levels of stress hormones and markers of inflammation after their course.

Previous studies have found that there are psychological and physical health benefits to mindfulness meditation and some therapists already use the practice to treat people who have anxiety. However, many previous studies of meditation compared groups of people who meditated to groups of people who did nothing. This means that any benefit of meditation seen in such studies could be due to the placebo effect resulting from people feeling that the treatment works rather than any physiological effect of the treatment.

In the new study, 89 participants who had previously been diagnosed with generalized anxiety disorder (GAD) were randomly assigned to take either the mindfulness meditation course or a stress-management education course. That course included lessons on ways to reduce stress though overall health and wellness, such as good nutrition, healthy sleep habits and time management.

Before and after the courses, participants underwent a laboratory test designed to make people feel stressed. They were asked to give a speech in front of "evaluators" dressed in white coats, with only a few minutes to prepare, and then were asked to do mental arithmetic. The researchers collected blood samples before and after the test, analyzing the blood for several biological markers of stress, including the stress hormone adrenocorticotropic hormone (ACTH), as well as the proteins IL-6 and TNF-alpha, which are markers of inflammation.

After the course, participants in the meditation group showed reductions in their levels of ACTH, IL-6 and TNF-alpha during the stress test, compared with the levels before they took the course. In contrast, the participants who took the stress management education course showed an increase in levels of these markers on their second stress test, compared to the first. That result suggests that these participants were even more anxious when they took the test a second time.

The findings suggest that mindfulness meditation may be a helpful strategy to decrease biological stress reactivity in people with anxiety disorder, but the scientists noted that future studies should look at the effect of meditation on "real-life" stress, rather than stress created during a lab experiment.

Well, no time like now for you to perform that "real-life" experiment! The term meditation refers to a broad variety of practices that includes techniques designed to promote relaxation, develop compassion, love, patience, generosity, and build internal energy or life force. The word meditation carries different meanings in different contexts. Meditation has been practiced since antiquity as a component of numerous religious traditions and beliefs.

Meditation often involves an internal effort to self-regulate the mind in some way. Meditation is also used to clear the mind and ease many health concerns, such as high blood pressure, depression, and anxiety. Meditation has a calming effect and directs awareness inward until pure "Awareness" is achieved.

Awareness in this context is not simply mental awareness of being present from the "egoistic" perspective. Here it is an awareness of the unity of life energy and being part of that. Many who experience this describe it as, "being awake inside without being aware of anything except awareness itself."

In brief, there are dozens of specific styles of meditation practice, and many different types of activity commonly referred to as meditative practices. It would be best to explore and find one you like. You can try different kinds of meditation.

For me using the binaural technology pioneered by Bob Monroe proved to a real shortcut. There are many producers of binaural sound products and even website where you can create your own tracks for free. I don't recommend a particular kind or producer, but DO strongly recommend you use it to help you get started. If you find you can enter a meditative state easily without using it, you should stop to prevent it from becoming a crutch that you don't need.

After intensively using it in conjunction with several types of meditation, I found two that I did particularly liked. One was a sitting type and the other an active form. My wife prefers to lie down and that has proven very effective for her. One particular activity you can try during meditation is to aim at effortlessly sustaining a single-pointed concentration of awareness while in meditation. Tom Campbell often refers to this as the "point of consciousness."

The only specific type of meditative technique I will teach in this book is related to this "point of consciousness" type and I call it the "Inner Sun." I came up with it after going to Cambodia on summer vacation with my buddy (the ghost witness) from Taiwan after he graduated Harvard Law. We had arranged to see the sunrise over the *Angkor Wat* temple complex and got up at 4:00 a.m. to drive out there. For once, a touristy thing actually was not overrated. The experience inspired me to formulate what I have come to call the Inner Sun practice.

You can do this either while sitting or lying down, but generally it is done in bed before sleep. It is excellent as a method help people fall asleep if they have trouble doing so. I have offered this technique to a number of people for precisely that, and except for one, it helped them to get to sleep very quickly. The one person it did not help sleep, it helped much more in another way. She went through the sun and into an amazing OBE.

I also experienced what I can only term OBEs shortly after I consistently practiced doing the Inner Sun before falling asleep. In hindsight, I can see that many people, including myself, were having these types of experiences before their body, emotions and mind were ready and became frightened. The fear made the experience unpleasant even if it would not have been had they been more conscious of what was really happening.

I had wanted to try going "out of body" ever since reading about it in Bob Monroe's books, but residual fear kept me from going for it. Eventually I felt I had to try it for myself, and in August of 2015, I told my wife I would try to do it. She was a bit cautious, believing that OBE's were just variations of the more lucid dream like experiences that she was familiar with. Not knowing what to expect despite Bob's books, Tom's videos, so many other things I have studied, I finally just went for it.

Amazingly, the very first time I tried, I succeeded beyond any of my wildest imaginings.

My target was one of the shadowy figures in my memory that I first encountered near Kailua Bay in Hawaii, then later in a mountain cabin in Japan, and then the last time on the shores of Lake Tahoe. I always assumed they must have been extraterrestrials of some kind since the first encounter happened shortly after I saw a metallic UFO with my Korean girlfriend in a park in Tokyo.

It would divert too much from the purpose here to go into all the details, but let me say that, to my surprise, when I went to look for the "extraterrestrials" somewhere "out there," I was shown a place somewhere within the Earth itself...

The Inner Sun Practice

Before beginning, remember that the practice is to imagine climbing a stepped pyramid in utter darkness to see the rise of the morning sun at the top of the pyramid. Prepare your mind to pay attention... within. Try imagining a virtual reality first person point of view video game...

Start by doing a full body relaxation routine. Concentrate on each muscle group and mindfully check that it is fully relaxed. Do this slowly all the way down the body from the head, then after taking several slow deep breaths, work your way back up the body, checking for any tension that you are still holding onto.

Once you feel fully relaxed. Begin to imagine climbing using both your arms and legs. It might help to get into the imagery to feel the wind or hear the sound of wind in your imagination.

When you are able to feel your attention becoming drawn into the imagined body rather than your sensory body, continue a bit then imagine coming to the top.

Imagine you are now resting and relaxed on the top of the pyramid...

Imagine your emotion of anticipation...

Imagine your intellect scanning the darkness for the first glimmer of the sun...

Imagine waiting to be glimpse the faint light of the "crack of dawn"…

Remain relaxed in this state of imagined patient anticipation…

When I first began to do this myself, it was mainly to help me fall asleep. Then one time, instead of falling asleep, I saw a glimmer of light from behind my closed eyes. The surprise made me wake up. I tried it again, and again I saw what looked like flashes of sunlight behind dark clouds, and I knew it was something I could get better at with practice. As time went on and I stayed with it, I did get better. It was hard to see at first and most of time, I would just fall asleep before seeing anything as the technique is very effective for doing that.

Slowly, I began to get the hang of it, and I could hold my attention longer and longer. With practice, I could stay conscious and wait for the sun to come out and eventually I could look directly into the sun as it rose fully without any glare or pain. I saw what I imagine the full sun would look like if I had eyes that could withstand it. The act of seeing the sun in my mind brought an overwhelming peace that stopped all thought. Even emotion seemed to cease, but there was a subtle mixture of emotions that felt like awe, elation, and anticipation. The sense of the body was long gone but I could still feel myself reaching out. There was only the sun and its light. I grasped the sun and the sun embraced me…

Well, there we are. A short story about how I made One Giant Leap into "the Inner Sun." I hope you have enjoyed this five part analogy of the human being as physical, emotional, intellectual, energetic, and…

When I was very young, thinking I was very clever and would stump my grandfather who seemed very ancient and wise (I was 7, he was 67.), I asked him, "What came before everything?"

"Tao," he said simply, "was before everything."

"But what was before that?" I asked impishly.

"The void that cannot be named, you name it, it is not it. If can you feel it, it is not it. If you can imagine it, it is not it. You cannot know anything about it."

"Why?"

"Because it is beyond anything"

"But… why?"

"Even if you could leap into it, you cannot remember. If you can remember, it is not it."

"How do I leap into it?"

He looked at me and smiled wistfully, knowing I will leave in a few years, perhaps never to return and most likely never to see him alive again.

"You ask a lot of questions."

Epilogue

I hesitated to add this epilogue but my wife convinced me. However, I want to make clear at the outset that I only acted on my own inner volition and do not feel any need to convince anyone else of my interpretation of what I perceived. My motivations to do what I did as a result were also mine alone and arose from within.

PERSONAL INTERLUDE – May 2016, San Francisco.

I am on my deck talking to my handyman about painting the house. "Hey, you see that intersection down there?" I nod. "I was there when that kid got killed. I saw everything. I am still traumatized. I need therapy!"

I remember seeing a makeshift memorial at that intersection about a year ago. It was not the first one there, and there have been lots of close calls at this busy intersection. I had noticed the small mound of flowers and candles driving by and assumed it was yet another fatal accident that we just seem to "get use to" as part of our vehicular culture… and as part of my inner focus, I had made a point to avoid most of what passes for news nowadays. I had no idea what had happened exactly or who was killed.

The eyewitness proceeds to tells me exactly what he saw…

It was Tuesday, May 12, 2015. It was a normal San Francisco morning, and a Chinese couple was seeing their young son off to school. The middle school student was on his way to class and was hit and killed by a Muni light rail train.

The boy was running to catch the train and while in the crosswalk across San Jose Avenue just before 8:30 a.m., a car and an SUV assuming the boy

would see them and they could speed through braked suddenly to avoid him.
Somehow, the boy panicked and leaped in front of the train that had started
moving forward.

He was pinned underneath the train. Sitting in his parked car, my
handyman saw what happened and hears the mother's screams. He sees her
desperate effort to save the boy pinned under the train.

"She was literally trying to push the train. Actually, she was trying to push
the train and pull him out from under because she saw him moving. The father
was there too. They were hysterical afterwards."

I can't stop thinking about the poor child who died just around a year ago
from the moment I first hear about it. Right away, I went to search for more
information based on the location and date of the accident as my handyman
had no recollection of the name of the child.

As I sat at the computer, I thought to myself why not meditate on the
meaning of hearing that story before I search?

I closed my eyes and before I had time to enter a relaxed state, much less
a meditative one, a voice in my head says, "Andy... saw..." My eyes pop back
open.

Well, that was new!

The young man's name was Andrew Wu. The internet confirmed
everything I had been told, and I even saw my handyman interviewed in
one of the TV reports. It was heartbreaking...

After getting a strong feeling of connection to Andy from reading
about his tragic death, I intentionally sought out information on him in
deep meditation. And information came to me. Again, I only report what
I recollect of seeing and do not insist that indeed his "ghost" was doing
such and such.

I saw... Andy riding endlessly on the train... he is being pushed around
by older denizens of the same abode... he tries to hide and stay away from
them... He is so scared and not happy... He can see me...

I want to help you. I don't know how...

I thought about contacting the Spiritualist Society. I spoke to one Baha'i friend and she shared some of her own experiences along similar lines. I told my wife as soon as I made "contact," but she had as little idea what to do next as I did.

Ultimately, I went... within.

Slowly, the things that I could do that might help started to be able to intuit. Some took effort, some cost money, but it was nothing too difficult. Externally, I decided I knew what I was doing and did not share my specific activities even with my wife beyond telling her that I was pleasing myself doing something for Andy's memory.

Internally, I did what I wanted to do from all aspects of my being.

A few days after I completed the last of the three things that I intuited might help him go beyond where he was, I went into a deep meditation and intended to see Andy... Somehow I already knew it would be the last time...

I see Andy... he is on an empty train by himself. He seems excited and happy... the train is moving rapidly towards a tunnel full of light... he turns towards me smiling and waves...

Meditations

On the night I finished this book, I cast the "I-Ching" Oracle three times, asking for a blessing, a guide and a forecast for you, its future readers. These are the answers that came back. None had "moving lines," so your future is coming into clear focus...

THE WELL

There is a Source common to us all. Jung named it the Collective Unconscious. Others hail it as God within. Inside each of us are dreamlike symbols and archetypes, emotions and instincts that we share with every other human being. When we feel a lonely separateness from others, it is not because this "Well" within has dried up, but because we have lost the means to reach its waters.

You need to reclaim the tools necessary to penetrate to the depths of your fellows. Then the bonds you build will be as timeless and inexhaustible as the Well that nourishes them.

ENDURANCE

Endurance is the key to success in this situation. However, durability is not synonymous with stone-like rigidity. True resilience requires a flexibility that allows adaptation to any adverse condition, while still remaining true to the core. Can you maintain your integrity under any circumstance? Can you influence the situation without giving opposing forces anything to resist? Then you will endure to reach your goal.

INNOCENCE

This is a time of interchange between a mentor and pupil. Whether you are the teacher or the student, it is a time of companionship along a mutual path, the eternal, cyclical path of the mentor/student relationship -- a mentor is merely a more seasoned pupil, further along on the journey.

A pupil holds within himself the seed of a future Master.

Printed in the United States
By Bookmasters